The Matthew 6:33 Principle

It is with deep respect and honor that I acknowledge Gaylon and Debbie Childers as pillars in our ministry. The Holy Spirit places helpers and encouragers in the lives of God's ministers. These two people have been there with full support, in every situation.

If another "Book of Acts" was being written, Gaylon and Debbie would be in it, as helpers in the kingdom of God

— *Sam Jordan, Ph.D.*

The Matthew 6:33 Principle

Turning Your Heart to the Kingdom of God

SAM JORDAN, PH.D.

SYREN BOOK COMPANY
Minneapolis

Most Syren Books are available at special quantity discounts for bulk purchases for sales promotions, premiums, fund-raising, and educational needs. For details, write

    Syren Book Company
    Special Sales Department
    5120 Cedar Lake Road
    Minneapolis, MN 55416

Copyright © 2005 by Sam Jordan

All rights reserved. No part of this publication may be reproduced in any manner whatsoever without the prior written permission of the publisher.

Published by
Syren Book Company
5120 Cedar Lake Road
Minneapolis, MN 55416

Printed in the United States of America on acid-free paper

ISBN-13: 978-0-929636-46-7
ISBN-10: 0-929636-46-5

LCCN 2005927226

Cover design by Kyle G. Hunter
Book design by Rachel Holscher

To order additional copies of this book see the form at the back of this book or go to www.itascabooks.com

(CONTENTS)

	Preamble	VII
	Preface	IX
CHAPTER ONE	Matthew 6:1–34	3
CHAPTER TWO	His Righteousness	9
CHAPTER THREE	These Things Shall Be Added	16
CHAPTER FOUR	Supernaturally Natural	19
CHAPTER FIVE	The Law of Reciprocity	23
CHAPTER SIX	Born with a Purpose	31
CHAPTER SEVEN	Human Traits	38
CHAPTER EIGHT	The Subject of Money and Success	52
CHAPTER NINE	The Kingdom of God in Contradistinction to the Kingdom of Heaven	58
CHAPTER TEN	The Church	67
CHAPTER ELEVEN	Faith	73
CHAPTER TWELVE	The Two Minds	78
CHAPTER THIRTEEN	What Is My Gift?	85
CHAPTER FOURTEEN	The Law of Life	88
CHAPTER FIFTEEN	The Snubbing Post	93
CHAPTER SIXTEEN	Vessel to Honor, Vessel to Dishonor	98
CHAPTER SEVENTEEN	Security	101

(PREAMBLE)

> Securing the future is a paramount desire of humanity.

We human beings were created in the image of God (Genesis 1:26–27), which means we have been endowed with many attributes of God. Among the myriad characteristics that God did *not* endow us with was the ability to know the future. Having knowledge of the future was put off limits to us (Deuteronomy 18:10–12; 29:29). God has given a veiled glimpse of the future through prophecy, but that glimpse does not include knowledge of what is in store for us as persons.

A desire for future security is, arguably, our foremost search. However, seeking security based upon definitive information leaves us with only methods of contingency. This brings us face-to-face with situations confronting the world today:

- Homeland security
- Social security
- Health security
- Job security
- Retirement security
- Environmental security
- Nuclear security
- Security from terrorist attacks
- Eternal security

The list is only partial, but it is enough for us to realize the cry of humanity. Fear is the dominating factor surrounding the possibilities. Many of our fears are subjective, but they are nonetheless very real to the troubled soul.

Almighty God knows the beginning to the end (Alpha and Omega, Revelation 1:8). Why did He leave us in the dark on this important subject? Great strides have been made in education and technology, but we are no closer to unlocking the secrets of the future.

God has reserved that mystery unto Himself. However, He has made provisions for His followers that include protection, guidance, wisdom, and the revelation of many secret things (Psalms 25:10–14; 91:1–16; Daniel 2:19–22).

These are the reasons for this treatise. I trust that as you read, the Holy Spirit will enlighten you regarding some perplexing questions.

(PREFACE)

Every book should have a clearly stated purpose for existing. Such is the case with this writing. My foundational resolve here is to project a concept, namely, that God has an explicit plan for all creation. Moreover, He supplies the necessary requirements to fulfill His purpose. To receive God's provision, the thing created must adhere to its objective. If the creation is a human being, the same concept holds true.

Therefore, virtually all creation fulfills God's expectation, except humankind. God formed us as free moral beings, capable of distinguishing between right and wrong. Having God's favor hinges upon making the right choices, but the Bible historically reveals that we humans are anomalous in our views and action.

God designed a plan to bring us back into His favor in Christ Jesus, and once again be what God created us to be, thus having God's anointing of supply and blessings. Jesus Christ came to this earth with God's message to all humankind, teaching, showing, and literally proving that it is God's desire to bless His children with a good life. There is a prescribed method that must be followed—and that method forms the nucleus of this book.

The Matthew 6:33 Principle: Turning Your Heart to the Kingdom of God is a sequel to my memoir, *From Religion to Rebellion to Relationship* (St. Paul: Western Home Books, 2005). It is my hope that many things described in that earlier book will be made more understandable by reading this one.

God brought me from a life of poverty, ignorance, and rebellion to one of understanding, obedience, and abundance. The following pages share the truth and revelation that turned my heart and life around. It is my prayer that as you explore the following concepts you, too, shall be blessed.

The Matthew 6:33 Principle

(CHAPTER ONE)

Matthew 6:1–34

> But seek ye first the kingdom of God and His righteousness, and all these things shall be added unto you. (MATTHEW 6:33)

This is the scripture that God used to capture my attention. My natural desire was to have the material things referred to in the latter part of Matthew 6:33: "All these things shall be added unto you." "All these things" refers to the topic discussed in Matthew 6—material goods.

When I first encountered this passage, I was interested in only the material aspects of life, but as I read the whole of chapter 6 I experienced a revelation that changed my perspective. It dawned on me that God had created every living thing for a purpose. If the thing created fulfilled the created purpose, it was God's promise to supply the necessary provisions. This revelation changed my worldview completely.

Before any of us can attain a concrete view of life, there must be an awareness of why we exist. Without that comprehension, life and all the bumps along its path will create confusion, discouragement, and eventual failure. Philosophers have debated this question for centuries.

William James, in *The Varieties of Religious Experience* (New York: Longman, 1902), wrote: "Religion in the broadest sense consists of the belief that there is an unseen order, and that our supreme good lies in harmoniously adjusting ourselves thereto" (p. 53).

Perhaps Mr. James didn't know Christ personally, but he did have a concept of aligning oneself with the designed purpose for which we exist: it would bring harmony into our lives. It's virtually impossible to defeat anyone who has a clear sense of purpose (Psalm 1:2–3: "But his delight is in the law of the Lord, and on His law he meditates day and night. He is like a tree planted by streams of water, which yields its fruit in season and whose leaf does not wither. Whatever he does prospers" [unless noted, all passages are quoted from the New International Version of the Holy Bible]).

God knows precisely where we are at all times. He knows our thoughts, our concepts, and what forces brought us to our way of life. He is cognizant of what is needed to get our attention. God created us and "knows our frame" (Psalm 103:14: "For He knows how we are formed, He remembers that we are dust"). Regardless, the crucial interest in life shall dictate nearly all attention. When God desires to speak to each of us, He will generally focus on our main interest.

The Bible is an astounding book of psychology that goes directly to the heart of an underlying flaw. Nothing is hidden from God. We can manipulate and fool people, but we can't circumvent God's Word, which is sharper than a two-edged sword (Hebrews 4:12).

Matthew 6:1–8 converges on the most common human motivation—to be seen and admired by other people. Even in religious endeavors, we seek to please others—as if what they think is going to change the outcome of life.

Jesus is saying that if being admired is our motive for religious activity, God will not bless the effort. People may admire the behavior, but that would be the extent of the blessing. If we want God's help in life, we must search out what pleases Him and adjust our thinking to please Him.

In verses 6–8 Jesus is addressing prayer, supposedly to God the Father, but He condemns the long flowery prayer filled with eloquence and rhetoric. Why? Because that sort of praying is aimed at impressing human beings.

We want to impress God with our heartfelt needs. We must have faith in Him. He already knows our needs, but He wants us to articulate them. God is concerned with sincerity and desires to know that we are confident He will hear us when we pray.

As I studied chapter 6 I began realizing how wrong I had been in my views. I had wanted to separate myself from religion, thinking that to do so would make me appear tough and manly. Obviously, I thought that anyone adhering to Jesus Christ was weak, unmanly, and poor. That was the life I remembered while growing up.

I wanted a better way of life. I thought I could best find it outside Jesus Christ. Just how stupid can a person be? How does a thing like that happen to anyone? Minds are blinded by our enemy (2 Corinthians 4:4: "The god of this age has blinded the minds of unbelievers, so that they cannot see the light of the gospel of the glory of Christ, who is the image of God"). I thought I could be independent and find success and happiness on my own—that's human reasoning, and it is antithetical to God's way (Proverbs 3:5–6: "Trust in the Lord with all your heart and lean not on your own understanding; in all your ways acknowledge Him and He will make your paths straight").

There wasn't any doubt in my mind that God was real, or that Jesus Christ was who the Bible said He was. And I believed that the Holy Spirit indwelt a person who obeyed God's Word, literally. I really believed all these doctrines. But I also believed that to follow them I would have to reject any hope of being successful in life and shun all forms of entertainment.

This oversimplification of what it meant to be a Christian caused me to believe that a person who closely followed Jesus Christ was outside the mainstream of life and looked weak and sissified. I really didn't believe I could be prosperous if I trusted God. I simply did not know the nature of God and His promises.

When I read the sixth chapter of Matthew I received a revelation that turned my perspective upside down. The concept I received was that God created everything with a definitive purpose. If the thing created fulfilled the created purpose, then God supplied all necessities required—according to God's plan. That is the core teaching of Matthew 6:33.

Those who have a firm awareness that they are being used of the Lord in His kingdom will have faith that God will meet their needs. Any preacher, teacher, pastor, or individual who has found this secret in God has many events to report on how God has performed miracles in his or her life. God is not a respecter of persons; He will do the same for anyone who diligently seeks Him (Hebrews 11:6: "And without faith it is impossible to please God, because anyone who comes to Him must believe that He exists and that He rewards those who earnestly seek Him").

However, many of these miracles take place in such a fashion that it appears the people are lucky, simply in the right place at the right time. But if we are aware of God's Word and have faith to believe, then we realize that it's because the Holy Spirit is behind the scenes, orchestrating things, that the miracle occurs.

There is a law of reciprocity, and God ordained the system. It is the law of sowing and reaping. Everything in life seems to work on that premise. We must sow before we can harvest. It would be asinine to expect a harvest unless we planted or sowed first. Because God created the system, He has made that law clearly understood in the Bible.

Many folks attend church and claim Christ as their savior, but they do not adhere to that predominant principle. They want to receive without sowing first. Gambling comes under this method of gaining without producing anything helpful.

Let's read what God's Word has to say on the matter. Galatians 6:7–9, for example, tells us that God cannot be cheated, we cannot circumvent the condition that we reap where we sow ("Do not be deceived: God cannot be mocked. A man reaps what he sows. The one who sows to please his sinful nature, from that nature will reap destruction; the one who sows to please the Spirit, from the Spirit will reap eternal life. Let us not become weary in doing good, for at the proper time we will reap a harvest if we do not give up"). The Bible is filled with scriptures that address the subject.

Look at Luke 6:38: "'Give and it will be given to you. A good measure, pressed down, shaken together and running over, will be poured into your lap. For with the measure you use, it will be measured to you.'" If we give, we shall receive in abundant return, according to the generosity we project, but notice where the return comes from: it comes from a natural source (humankind). It appears that human beings in some way are producing the increase. In fact, however, it's the Holy Spirit working behind the scenes, causing it to happen. It is simply the law of God. It's important to grasp the distinction that even though God is causing events to unfold, the events are being carried out by human effort.

Most great miracles from God come about similar to this illustration, because God works with our laws of time, cause, and effect.

Sometimes there are miracles that don't require time, cause, and effect. They happen instantaneously, simply because God wants them to occur. This fact conveys to us the sovereignty of God. There is nothing we can do to bring the miracle about or prevent it from happening.

We must not try to place God in a box. God does not check with us when He desires to handle a situation. Our responsibility is to have faith in God. We must believe that He knows best for our lives and that whatever He does is for our good (Jeremiah 29:11: "'For I know the plans I have for you,' declares the Lord, 'plans to prosper you and not to harm you, plans to give you hope and a future'").

Habakkuk 3:17–18 describes an attitude that we should have toward God:

> Although the fig tree shall not blossom, neither shall fruit be in the vines; the labor of the olive shall fail and the fields shall yield no food; and there shall be no herd in the stalls; yet I will rejoice in the Lord, I will rejoice in the God of my salvation.

This scripture encapsulates the focus we should have in our relationship with God. Our love for and devotion to Him should not be affected positively or negatively by anything we encounter in life. There is an example I sometimes use to illustrate this point: "We don't stop breathing because of some disappointment in our life." God is closer than our breath. He is our life. We maintain our relationship with Him, no matter what.

God is "our heavenly Father." He knows what is best for our life in every situation. Sometimes it doesn't appear that way, but that's where faith comes into play. Our faith must be in Him.

(CHAPTER TWO)

His Righteousness

We have explored the first part of the admonition to seek first the kingdom of God, to make it a priority. Now we turn our attention to the second part of the exhortation: God's righteousness.

Notice how the complete teaching has three parts. Why? We are told to make the kingdom of God our priority, both in our own personal life and to further the development of God's kingdom on earth. The second part tells us how it must be done—through His righteousness. We don't have a vote in the matter; it must be done God's way.

The first part could be accomplished in numerous ways, depending upon our interpretation of the kingdom of God. Various religions seek to do this—Islam or Judaism, for instance. However, His righteousness identifies how it must be accomplished. Israel had a passion for God but not according to knowledge. The Hebrews were ignorant of God's righteousness and did not submit to the righteousness of God (Romans 10:3: "Since they did not know the righteousness that comes from God and sought to establish their own, they did not submit to God's righteousness").

Regardless of how hard we try to please God, we fail in our efforts, unless Jesus Christ is the center of our activity. He is our righteousness, and when we seek to further the kingdom of God it must be through Him. The only act that God recognizes is to accept Jesus Christ. God rejects all other efforts (Acts 4:12: "Salvation is found in no one else, for there is no other name under heaven given to men by which we must be saved").

Since Jesus Christ is our sole center of activity, we must know precisely what Jesus commands us to do to further the kingdom of God. How do we get that information? There are two major sources:

+ God's Word, the Bible; and
+ The Holy Spirit.

Before the New Covenant (New Testament), Israel didn't have the resource we have had for the past two thousand years. The New Covenant includes the Holy Spirit dwelling within every child of God—Immanuel, God with us (Matthew 1:23: "'The virgin will be with child and will give birth to a son, and they will call him Immanuel'—which means, 'God with us'"). God is constantly with each believer. The promise to each believer was fulfilled after the day of Pentecost, when the Holy Spirit came. The Holy Spirit will direct our path in seeking the kingdom of God. Having the righteousness of God, in Christ Jesus, is an act of the Holy Spirit.

The Gospel of John, chapters 14–16, describes God's promise to us of the Holy Spirit, as a comforter and guide. Jesus Christ asked the Father to send this powerful person of the Godhead to dwell in each of us.

If we are not careful when we read the account in John, we might lean toward the Jesus-only concept, denying the Trinity. We must remember that the three—God the Father, God the Son, and God the Holy Spirit—are distinct yet unified personalities that work in absolute harmony.

Notice that in John 16:7–15, the Holy Spirit had not come at this point and Jesus promised to send Him (the Holy Spirit) after Jesus' departure. Jesus said the Holy Spirit would do certain things when He does come. Verses 7–11 detail the things the Holy Spirit will do in the world; verses 12–16 describe things the Holy Spirit will do for you and me, personally.

One of the things the Holy Spirit will do for us is to show us what Jesus Christ wants us to do in building the kingdom of God (John 16:14–15: "'He will bring glory to me by taking from what is mine and making it known to you. All that belongs to the Father is mine. That is why I said the Spirit will take from what is mine and make it known to you'"). When we do what Jesus Christ asks us to do in pursuing the kingdom of God, we can expect God to make things work out in our lives according to His will (Romans 8:26–28: "And we know that in all things God works for good of those who love Him, who have been called according to His purpose").

This is the Matthew 6:33 principle.

Have you ever wondered why God answers some requests and seems to deny others? Many times they are petitions that seem valid and in line with God's Word. Perhaps it's because the request does not fit into His will at the moment. God sees the big picture and we do not. God wants to meet our needs, but there may be circumstances surrounding a situation that cause Him not to deliver an answer (1 John 5:14–15: "This is the confidence we have in approaching God: that if we ask anything according to His will, He hears us. And if we know that He hears us—whatever we ask—we know that we have what we asked of Him"). That is why the Holy Spirit is the key in asking God, because He knows the will of God (Romans 8:27: "And He who searches our hearts knows the mind of the Spirit, because the Spirit intercedes for the saints in accordance with God's will").

A faith preacher of days gone by, Smith Wigglesworth, said, "I may pray for a whole year on a matter, in order to get the Will of God, but when I have the Will of God on the subject, I will only pray a short time and it is granted, or rejected."

The will of God is paramount in living a "God-anointed life." The will of God is easily determined in some situations, for example:

- Receiving salvation, redemption, justification: God is not willing that anyone be lost but that all should come to repentance (2 Peter 3:9);
- Having faith or trust in Jesus Christ;
- Receiving the Holy Spirit into our lives;
- Being kind and considerate; and
- Forgiving others.

These are just a few areas of life about which we already know the mind of God because His Word declares His intention. We don't have to pray about the will of God in these matters; they are established.

(A word of caution, however: each of us can only receive these things for his or her own life. We cannot—I repeat, we cannot—force them on someone else.)

We referred to God's righteousness as the second part of the exhortation. We know we cannot earn our redemption, but after we are redeemed through faith in Jesus Christ, we can and should have acts of righteousness, acts and deeds that Christ created us for (Ephesians 2:10: "For we are God's workmanship, created in Christ Jesus to do good works, which God prepared in advance for us to do"). In Romans, *sanctification* is translated from the same Hebrew word as *holy*. It basically means to be set apart for a special purpose.

After we have been justified, redeemed by faith in Jesus Christ, then the Holy Spirit begins a process of sanctification. Little by little He changes us into Christlike characters, for the purpose of being effective witnesses to Jesus Christ. This is a process that continues throughout our lifetime.

The moment we accept Christ as our redeemer, we are justified before our heavenly Father, justified in our "position." It is important to understand this statement. It will help us comprehend many things in God's Word. Justification means that it is as if we had never sinned. Our place in Jesus Christ is complete (Colossians

2:10: "And you have been given fullness in Christ, who is the head over every power and authority").

This is not the end of the story, of course. The Holy Spirit starts His work of sanctification in our life to bring our life's activity, our nature and our character up to the level of our new position (Philippians 2:12–13: "Therefore, my dear friends, as you have obeyed—not only in my presence, but now much more in my absence—continue to work out your salvation with fear and trembling, for it is God who works in you to will and to act according to His good purpose"). We are fully aware that Paul is not referring to our being redeemed—it is impossible to be redeemed by works or human effort (Ephesians 2:8–9: "For it is by grace you have been saved, through faith—and this not from yourselves, it is the gift of God—not by works, so that no one can boast"). Paul is talking about our life's activities coming up to the standard of our redeemed position. This is the work of the Holy Spirit and the believer taking place together. This interpretation should throw some understanding on Paul's discourse in Romans 7:15–25. Jesus Christ, not our religious activities, is our righteousness. There will be deeds of righteousness initiated by the Holy Spirit, emerging from our life.

It's interesting to note in Revelation 19:8 that we shall be granted fine, clean, white linen for the marriage supper of the Lamb: "Fine linen, bright and clean, was given her to wear. (Fine linen stands for the righteous acts of the saints)." We receive a garment of righteousness through Jesus Christ; then we begin to do acts of righteousness motivated by the Holy Spirit.

We can never, in this life, come fully up to the level of our position in Christ Jesus. Human bodies are not equipped for perfection. That's the reason God has ordained that we receive resurrected bodies or translated bodies (1 Corinthians 15:50–57; 1 Thessalonians 4:13–18). God shall present to us bodies equipped for new life in eternity.

However, we should examine our lives periodically to see if we are making progress toward perfection under the tutorship of the Holy Spirit and God's Word. We should be closer to our new position than we were when we started.

What should we look for in our lives to determine our level of progress? There are many things about our characters that it shall be obvious to us have changed, especially when we measure our temperament against the Word of God.

The changes occur slowly and almost without our being aware of them. The progress is the outcropping of the Holy Spirit within us. We can impede the process by being obstinate and refusing to cooperate with the Holy Spirit's unction. Conversely, we can speed up sanctification by recognizing our flaws, in light of God's Word and the Holy Spirit's illumination, and by asking God to help us overcome our contrary nature. We must have the desire to change.

Everything about our salvation begins with accepting Jesus Christ. He gives to us right standing with our heavenly Father, after which the Holy Spirit motivates us to perform deeds that are counted as deeds of righteousness. All is geared toward our becoming witnesses to Jesus Christ, building the kingdom of God on earth, through His righteousness.

Before we leave the topic of God's righteousness, there is something more to be said about our lives concerning His righteousness.

> Blessed are they who do hunger and thirst after righteousness, for they shall be filled. (Matthew 5:6)

This is one of the beatific characteristics promised by Jesus Christ in the Sermon on the Mount. As you read each of these promises, it becomes clear that they are not attainable by natural ability. Therefore, it is acts of the Holy Spirit that make them possible.

This brings up an interesting question: how does a person acquire a hunger for righteousness?

Many folks who accept Jesus Christ as savior do so to satisfy some physical or emotional need, and they really don't have a desire for righteousness. They may only want a solution to an immediate problem. They may only want a fire insurance policy against hell.

It appears that God in His love for us will accept us when we have faith and confess our reception of Jesus Christ (Romans 10:9–13). Through our knowledge of God's Word we know that Jesus Christ is our righteousness (1 Corinthians 1:30). Yet, there isn't necessarily that deep hunger for righteousness.

How do we receive a deep hunger for God's righteousness? Jesus answers that question in Matthew 7:7–8.

We must ask God for a supernatural love for Jesus Christ and His righteousness and to create a hunger within us: "When we hunger and thirst after righteousness, we shall be filled" (Matthew 5:6). With this answer comes a relationship with Christ that surpasses human understanding.

If we really want to be filled, we must ask, knock, and seek. This approach certainly indicates more than a passing fancy; it means an ongoing process.

We are designed to attain almost anything that the heart is set on accomplishing. Determining to pursue a goal will generally produce results, providing the desire is not tainted with double-mindedness. Many scriptures confirm this axiom (Psalm 1:2–3; Luke 6:38; Mark 11:23–24). Most failures in life are the result of weak determination and lack of commitment.

(CHAPTER THREE)

These Things Shall Be Added

Material things attract the attention of most people; we are physically oriented beings. Our approach to God, most of the time, concerns material matters. Matthew 6 speaks to our material needs. God already knows we require these things before we ask Him for them. He is reminding us that prioritizing our life is important if we are going to have His support.

I understand this exhortation in the following way:

- God made everything with a purpose, and if everything He made does what it is designed to do, then God will provide what is necessary to accomplish the activity.
- The preceding concept started me searching to find the purpose for which God made us. I found it in Ecclesiastes 12:13. "The conclusion of the whole matter: Fear God and keep His commandments, for this is the whole duty of man."
- The purpose for which God blesses us financially: to establish God's covenant (Deuteronomy 8:18). God gives us power to obtain wealth, not for our pleasure but to further the kingdom of God.

- When our first concern is God's kingdom, beautiful things happen in our lives.
- Tithing and offerings are important functions of worship.

Financial means are required for almost anything we do in life. We devote a large part of our lives to earning money. In many cases it is the most important commodity we seek. We are reluctant to part with our money unless we receive value in return. When we are confronted with matters concerning God's work, finding value received escapes us, and we therefore have a tendency to ignore the Bible's teaching on the subject. We will put a little into the church, but not in a way that could be classified as putting God's work first. It takes a firm faith to continually give money to God's work.

A working relationship with Jesus Christ requires knowing Him on a personal basis—knowing His interests, knowing what He wants to accomplish. Such a relationship should involve the conviction that Jesus Christ knows us personally and that He knows what we desire to accomplish. If we honestly know that our ambition is different from Christ's plan, then the relationship is strained. A relationship that is not relaxed will result in a hampered faith.

Seeking first the kingdom of God and His righteousness will result in a live faith. Seeking His kingdom first will give us an assurance of fulfillment of the promise that "all these things shall be added unto us." Having this confidence constitutes a great recompense of reward (Hebrews 10:35–36: "Cast not away, therefore, your confidence, which hath great recompense of reward. For you have need of patience that, after ye have done the will of God, you might receive the promise"). We must apply patience to receive the promise.

It is our responsibility to know what seeking first the kingdom of God and His righteousness entails and then pursuing that course of action. If your interpretation of this action is the same as mine, it shall come down to helping Jesus Christ fulfill His mission, namely, seeking out the lost (Luke 19:10: "'For the Son of Man came to seek and to save what was lost'"). Since the church is the body of Christ, then the church's mission and the head are one and the same—Jesus Christ.

Every believer has been given a measure of faith and a gift to be used to further the Kingdom of God (Romans 12:3–16). God wants us to realize that each of us has a ministry of reconciliation (2 Corinthians 5:17–20).

Our gift may seem insignificant compared to those of other folks in the church, but we should resist making comparisons. We should be obedient to the Holy Spirit's anointing in our life (Matthew 25:14–27).

Each born-again believer earning money has a responsibility to help finance the work of God. The church body where we attend must have funds to function; thus, it behooves each of us to help support it, as unto the Lord Jesus Christ. We are not to dictate where the money is used; that responsibility belongs to the person with a gift of handling church finance. We have done our part when we tithe and give offerings. If any of us slacks off paying tithes and offerings, we should read Malachi 3:7–11. We might find there why we are struggling in our financial lives.

Each of us must decide where we fit into the picture of helping Jesus Christ accomplish His purpose. The Holy Spirit will guide us in that decision. We must be faithful to our responsibility in order to be confident that God will make everything work out in our lives (Romans 8:28).

Meditating on the concept I have presented may give the impression that Jesus Christ is a hard taskmaster. Nothing could be further from the truth. Jesus was thinking of each and every one of us when He said, "Come unto me all you that labor and are heavy laden and I will give you rest for your souls." He also said that His burdens are light (Matthew 11:28–30). God wants ours to be lives of abundance, filled with peace and joy. He knows that the only way for that to happen is to be obedient to His purpose and live according to His righteousness. God causes things to be added unto us.

(CHAPTER FOUR)

Supernaturally Natural

Many speakers and writers have a tendency to relate how God has blessed their lives, without sharing the whole story. They make events sound as though they happened immediately, similar to hitting the lottery. We don't intend to come across that way. We simply don't have time to develop the complete picture. Some answers from God come with a time lapse, but in relating the event we many times leave out the time element. The answer did come, but not immediately.

Some events are absolutely miraculous, almost unbelievable. However, most changes came about naturally. I refer to them as "supernaturally natural." God orchestrates the changes, but there's generally a natural process involved. Explaining what I mean by "supernaturally natural" may revolutionize some people's thinking about living successfully in God.

Most things in life operate on a progressive system (cause and effect). It's easy for us to overlook that God uses progressive methods when dealing with us. After all, He is God and can make things appear at His whim. There are people in Christian circles who believe that if they have enough faith they can activate God to wiggle His little finger (so to speak) and a miracle will occur, circumventing the natural process.

Reading biblical accounts of Jesus' miracles inspires us to think we can imitate His deeds and believe that we should aspire to having enough faith to perform such actions. We honestly want to follow in Jesus' footsteps. Therefore, if He performed these miracles, we should be able to perform them also.

Some things were intended for only Jesus Christ to perform. I shall enumerate a few and explain why they were designed for Him alone.

- Jesus Christ had the Holy Spirit without measure (John 3:34: "'For He whom God hath sent speaketh the words of God; for God giveth not the Spirit by measure *unto Him*'").

No human being has the Holy Spirit without measure.

- Jesus Christ knew the mind of the Father in His every action (Romans 8:26–27).

We don't always know the mind of the Father.

- Jesus Christ only did what the Father showed Him to do, and He did it exactly as the Father told Him (John 5:19: "Jesus gave them this answer: 'I tell you the truth, the Son can do nothing by himself; he can do only what he sees his Father doing, because whatever the Father does the Son also does'").

It would be great if we could function this way, but we rarely do.

- The Father revealed things to Jesus Christ as to no one else (John 5:20: "'For the Father loves the Son and shows him all he does. Yes, to your amazement he will show him even greater things than these'").

Jesus came for the purpose of starting a whole new way of life—the church.

- The Father endowed Jesus with power for the purpose of causing humanity to marvel (John 5:20).

Jesus' purpose was to reveal a supernatural power that supersedes this present life.

- Jesus Christ exercised no will of His own. He followed the Father's agenda—He did only the will of the Father (John 5:30: "'By myself I can do nothing; I judge only as I hear, and my judgment is just, for I seek not to please myself but him who sent me'").

We have a will and it's rarely in line with the Father's will. We generally have our own agenda. The preceding are only a few scripture passages in which Jesus accomplished things that no other human being can produce.

Sometimes we ask God for something that is directly in line with His perfect will. And if we do it precisely as God directs us, then we will see a miracle that astounds us (1 John 5:14–15). We would like this to be the norm, but we are human and our thinking is not always in line with God's will.

Most of our prayers are built around our desires. Many times we try to manipulate God's Word to fit our request, but there are so many variables surrounding our requests, such as timing, other personalities involved, and how the ultimate outcome will affect our future. Only God knows the future. Therefore, most of our requests miss the perfect will of God as a result of our human limitations.

Having said all this, shouldn't we pray and ask God for miracles? Of course we should. And at times we see miracles. We ask and then leave the results in the hands of God. God works out the results in due season (Galatians 6:9: "Let us not become weary in doing good, for at the proper time we will reap a harvest if we do not give up").

The primary purpose of this chapter has been to remind us that we are physical human beings with the Holy Spirit within. The purpose of the Holy Spirit in our lives is twofold:

- To bring us into new life (to be born again) (Romans 8:9).
- To cause us to be witnesses to Jesus Christ (Acts 1:8: "But you will receive power when the Holy Spirit comes on you; and you will be my witnesses in Jerusalem, and in all Judea and Samaria, and to the ends of the earth").

Therefore, our everyday activity is dedicated to God as His agents on earth. Although our activities are physical, the Holy Spirit is directing our daily regimen. Christ-centered individuals should be cognizant of life being supernaturally natural, even when we are not fully aware of His presence (Acts 17:28: "For in him we live and move and have our being. As some of your own poets have said, 'We are his offspring'").

Little by little our soul is trained (our emotions, our will, our intellects—our desires) to put Christ and His kingdom first. *This is the Matthew 6:33 principle*. This change does not occur immediately upon conversion. It is developed over a period of time, under the auspices of the Holy Spirit. The pull of worldly desires begins to fade, and the kingdom of God and His righteousness grows brighter. We still have natural needs, of course, but God is supernaturally causing those needs to be met.

(CHAPTER FIVE)

The Law of Reciprocity

(Galatians 6:7–9)

The Word of God, in this passage, is speaking about spiritual conditions. However, the same law is in operation in all of creation. It goes without saying that if we plant corn, we receive corn in return. It we sow love, we receive love, and so forth. This is the law of reciprocity.

The law of reciprocity is in operation on earth. God created the law of sowing and reaping for us so that we would learn and obey (Galatians 6:7–9). The law of reciprocity does not lend itself to what we think of as a miracle. We want God to circumvent this law and meet our needs, *pronto*.

The law of reciprocity is a natural law, and nearly everything on Planet earth operates on this system. To have a good crop (prosperity), we must have a plan, work the plan, and overcome adversities that occur. The Holy Spirit works with this system, quickening our mortal bodies (Romans 8:11: "And if the Spirit of him who raised Jesus from the dead is living in you, he who raised Christ from the dead will also give life (or quicken) to your mortal bodies through his Spirit, who lives in you") and aiding us in our infirmities (Romans 8:26). We ask God in prayer to guide our action in our everyday activities, and the Holy Spirit will lead us to the appropriate action. All things will work to our good (Romans 8:28).

We must not judge results too quickly, for there may be an indefinite time lapse before seeing a positive side of our answer (Galatians 6:9)—assuming we do not become faint of heart (in other words, give up).

Our primary attitude is to have faith in God, to believe that He loves us and will work out the details of our life, if we ask Him and trust in Him. We must learn to have patience and refrain from trying to force God into doing our will. God has a systematic plan for life. The more we understand how God works, the better our life becomes. God created the world with these systems for our good.

We human beings attempt to circumvent many of God's systems, and when we do we can count on failure and difficulties. When understood and worked properly, God's systems function to our advantage. That's why it is so very important to know God's nature, as well as understand the systems that He has put into place. If these laws are violated, the outcome is not good.

When I first started learning to fly an airplane, for example, the instructor spent time teaching me about the effect of gravity. I soon leaned that if I attempted to violate that basic law, trouble was not far away. This illustration seems rather elementary, but it represents a God-directed law. All God's laws are just that certain. Some of His laws, however, take more time to reveal any violations.

On earth, we live on a time scale. Time requires a process of cause and effect. Therefore, as time progresses, success or failure follows, depending upon the seeds we sow (thinking and action). If we think incorrectly and act wrongly, we produce negative results. On the other hand, if we have proper thinking and proper action, we produce positive results. This concept may seem too simplistic, but basically it's the difference between a good life in contradistinction to one of defeat.

It is an innate human tendency to try to circumvent the process. That's precisely the enemy's main role, to encourage us to thwart God's plan (John 10:10: "'The thief [devil] comes to steal and kill and destroy; I have come that they may have life, and have it to the full'"). God placed in us the desire to have an abundant life. However, without the Holy Spirit, our thoughts and efforts to acquire an abundant life invariably turn toward destructive methods that seem right at the time (Proverbs 14:12). Human reasoning has a propensity toward:

- Lust
- Self-centeredness
- Self-gratification
- Jealousy
- Dishonesty

Galatians 5:17–21 describes many of these conditions.

Turning to Jesus Christ makes the Holy Spirit available to us, to direct and guide our decisions so that we don't rely on human reasoning for our future (Proverbs 3:1–10). When our bent is toward Jesus Christ and our trust is in God, we are headed for a successful, abundant, and peaceful existence (Psalm 1:2–3).

A young fellow told me one day, "Trusting God and living by the Word of God has worked for you, but it hasn't worked for me."

This young fellow was like many folks. He had tried God's way, for a short time, as though it were a formula, but he did not see any results. His mistake was in his concept of trying God's way—we don't "try" God's way. It isn't a theorem, it's a way of life.

When we make a decision to live God's way, we live according to His Word, whether we see successful results or not (Habakkuk 3:17–19: "Though the fig tree does not bud and there are no grapes on the vines, though the olive crop fails and the fields produce no food, though there are no sheep in the pen and no cattle in the stalls, yet I will rejoice in the Lord, I will be joyful in God my Savior"). Our soul has been redeemed and lifted up, and we live by faith (Habakkuk 2:4: "but the righteous will live by his faith").

We must not forget the time element, the process of sowing and reaping (Galatians 6:7–9). We must not grow weary of living life God's way, even though we go through difficult times before we see positive results. It isn't an endurance test; it's a matter of having faith in God.

I grew up believing that if we lived close enough to God, we would live by miracles that circumvented the natural progressive system. I believed the occurrence of miracles in one's life was a sign of spirituality. I later came to understand that, with rare exceptions, it is not God's plan for us to live by miracles that circumvent natural processes.

At times, of course, it's necessary that a miracle supersede the natural process; maybe there is not time for a natural process to play out, or perhaps the natural process would not produce what God wants for us. When a miracle is needed to fulfill God's desire or will, then He will perform a process-defying miracle. We have all seen such things, but they are not the norm.

I don't believe God wants us to need miracles constantly. We are created with faculties designed to be trained and directed into a good and successful life. Suppose, for example, that it is God's plan for you to be a physician. It therefore would not be a miracle if you became one; it would happen as you trained to be a doctor. If God intended for you to be a physician, the Holy Spirit would help you in your effort. He is the guiding force in a child of God (John 16:13: "'But when He, the Spirit of truth, comes, He will guide you into all truth'"; James 1:3–5).

Many benefits that flow to a Spirit-directed life come in natural ways. They do not appear spiritual, but they are God directed and thus they are supernaturally natural. We can find no greater proof of this statement than when reading the Book of Esther. There is not one mention of God in the whole book, but the providential care of God is evident in the beautiful story.

Many Christians believe that if the Holy Spirit is involved, there must be something superspiritual and church oriented. Christians who hold that concept leave the action of the Holy Spirit at the church door when they exit the building. They could be considered hearers of God's Word rather than doers of the Word (James 1:22–25). We should be doers of the Word every day in order to be blessed. To be doers of the Word of God, we must take action in everyday life, not exclusively in church services. Under the leadership of the Holy Spirit and God's Word, our soul is trained, a little bit at a time. As time passes we find ourselves acting out our day-to-day activities with a Godly flavor.

God's enemy, Satan, has done an effective job of confusing the work of God. Many Christians believe that God's work is done by preachers, evangelists, teachers, and others. Of course, they do have a special call of God in their lives. However, God's plan is for His work to be carried on in ordinary life circumstances, by Christians who have no titles, directed by the Holy Spirit in the home, on the job, in school, and wherever people are.

It is the task of preachers, evangelists, teachers, and others to train believers for the ministry, not to make professionals out of them, but to equip them to do the work of God in everyday life (Ephesians 4:11–16). A distinction should not be made between ministry and the work of laypeople. We are all ministers of the Gospel. We are all workers together with the Lord (2 Corinthians 6:1). Every believer is given a gift to be used for building the kingdom of God (Romans 12:1–21).

Every believer with a bent toward Jesus Christ, praying and looking to God's Word for direction, will have the Holy Spirit as a guide. The gift that God has endowed you with may seem insignificant, compared to the gifts of other believers, but it is just as valuable to God's kingdom as any other person's gift (Colossians 3:17: "And whatever you do, whether in word or deed, do it all in the name of the Lord Jesus, giving thanks to God the Father through him").

I do not want to encourage bondage by suggesting that we must constantly be looking for a spiritual connotation in everything we do. I want to encourage the understanding that each of us is under the direction of the Holy Spirit at all times. We walk and have our movement in the Spirit of God in our everyday activities. If we hold this concept, it replaces religion with a relationship with Christ.

In developing as instruments of God whom the Holy Spirit can use as tools for the kingdom of God in any situation (Romans 6:11–13), we become epistles of Jesus Christ, letters that are not written on paper or carved in stone (2 Corinthians 3:2–3).

When we operate under this attitude, there's a danger of becoming "holier than thou." Assuming a pious demeanor quickly removes a person from God's use in dealing with people. We are and have only what the Holy Spirit gives us (2 Corinthians 3:5: "Not that we are competent in ourselves to claim anything for ourselves, but our competence comes from God"). Operating under the influence of the Holy Spirit develops the sort of character that is described in 1 Corinthians 13:1–7.

A person who is used by the Holy Spirit as an instrument of righteousness will have Godly wisdom, be slow to speak in retort, and kind in all situations. God uses the person described in Isaiah 57:15: "I dwell in the high and holy place, with him also who is of a contrite and humble spirit, to revive the spirit of the humble, and to revive the heart of the contrite ones."

Filling the role of an instrument of God does not fit normal human nature. It requires God's Word and the Holy Spirit to change a person into an image of Jesus Christ. It is God's plan to change each human being into a vessel that brings honor and glory to God. When that occurs, everything about our life takes on a different cast, but it doesn't happen instantaneously.

Isaiah 28:9–10 gives a clear picture of how this process happens. It's line upon line, precept upon precept, here a little, there a little. It's another way of saying it comes through training, the events of life, some hardships, some joys. It all adds up to a lifetime of placing oneself under the tutelage of the Holy Spirit.

Many followers of Jesus Christ do not want to be that dedicated, to give themselves over to lives of obedience. Humanity has an agenda. Whatever that agenda consists of, they seek to accomplish its fulfillment. Folks want God's blessing, but they aren't too interested in helping God fulfill His plan. Matthew 6:33 is the principle of bringing God's power into everyday activity.

The *human* view of life in Christ—boring church meetings, no earthly enjoyment or financial success—is a fallacy. God desires His people to enjoy life in abundance. However, He does not want us to forget Him in the flow of life. We must never lose sight of the fact that it is He who makes life possible. We can accomplish much in our search for a good life, without recognizing God in the matter. It's God's desire, however, that we recognize His hand in all of life and that we honor Him.

Recall Old Testament accounts of God's efforts to remind Israel of His involvement. Idols were God's greatest competition in the life of Israel. It's amazing as well as ludicrous how Israel continually sought inanimate objects to rely on and trust.

The only way we can make sense of their actions is to believe that God wanted to make an example of human nature. Romans 15:4 tells us that what was written long ago in scripture was for our learning. I do not question the validity of what occurred, literally, but the vast element of time, cultural changes, and the development of language make it difficult for us today to have a perspective on life so long ago.

Human nature, on the other hand, does not change. We all tend to forget that God is our source, even after He has blessed us with so much. We soon forget God's hand of supply and turn to inanimate objects for sustenance—money, jobs, education, and so on. God does use these aids, but they are only instruments in the hand of God.

A child of God must maintain the focus that God and God alone is our source. Material blessings are just that—blessings. Our life does not consist of those things (Luke 12:15). We must remember the reason God blesses us materially (Deuteronomy 8:18).

Once again we must recall Matthew 6:33 as the road map to a beautiful life. When God's wind is to our backs, everything in life works to our good (Romans 8:28). We must always be aware that life will have some clouds and road bumps, but God has promised to bring good to us out of the difficulties.

If we affirm and sustain this mind-set, life will hold great promises. God is behind all occurrences, watching over every detail of our lives. We are His flock, for whom He provides pasture (Psalm 100:3: "Know that the Lord is God. It is he who made us, and we are his, we are his people, the sheep of his pasture").

(CHAPTER SIX)

Born with a Purpose

> But ye are a chosen generation, a royal priesthood, a holy nation, a people of His own, that ye should show forth the praises of Him who hath called you out of darkness into the marvelous light. (1 PETER 2:9)

Showing praises to God encompasses more than singing songs. It incorporates various ways in which we can show those around us that He is real and that we trust in Him for our very existence. We are called to let the world know that there is a God who involves Himself in all our daily activities.

God has endowed us with a purpose. Therefore, we can expect His attention to every aspect of our lives, despite events that seem to indicate otherwise (Romans 8:28). With this kind of outlook on life, nothing can defeat us (Philippians 4:4–9; 1 Thessalonians 5:16–24).

I know that God loves me, but why doesn't an all-loving God meet my every need? We all ask this question. We must remember that He wants to supply our needs. Sometimes our needs become confused with wants, and desires can run contrary to God's will. God wants us to be pliable in His guidance. We have natural desires that frequently do not fit God's plan for our lives. When that discrepancy exists, God will not answer our petitions or prayers (1 John 5:14–15).

Understanding the question of why God does not grant all requests perhaps is wrapped in the will of God (1 John 5:14–15). We may be asking God for something He wants to give us, but He desires to teach us a lesson first. There can be numerous reasons for His delay, even though our request may be valid. For example, a person who smokes may be ill from the habit, and God may want to free the person from the habit before healing him or her. Many such situations could account for His delay. There are times we will never know God's reason for delaying an answer. He is our heavenly Father, and we must respect His action if He chooses not to reveal His reasoning.

People who claim the Pentecostal experience (baptism in the Holy Spirit, Acts 2:4) feel they have a leg up with God for miracles. I believe there are some folks who do, but perhaps not for the reason they think. The Holy Spirit is the only one who knows the mind or will of the Father; therefore, when a person prays in the Spirit on any matter, God does answer. It may not be the answer the person is looking for, however. There may be cases in which an individual praying in the Spirit may not be aware of what the Spirit is praying for. The Holy Spirit prays according to the will of God (Romans 8:26–27). Praying in the Holy Spirit has so many benefits when we are seeking to approach God (Jude 20: "But you, dear friends, build yourselves up in your holy faith and pray in the Holy Spirit").

Living a fulfilling life in Jesus Christ comes when we realize that God is more concerned about transforming our character rather than being at our beck and call to provide a life of ease (Ephesians 3:11–21). Matthew 6:33 points us toward the need to put God's kingdom and righteousness above our own desires. It is God's will that His kingdom be built on earth. If our activities are involved with building His kingdom, we can be sure that our requests are in line for answers (Luke 11:2), all in God's time and according to His method and plan.

Through a billboard depiction of Matthew 6:33, which I believe God put in my path at an especially desperate time, I became aware of God's promise of a better life for me and my family. I soon came to realize, however, that there were going to be requirements on my part. There had to be changes in my character before an abundant life was mine. The Holy Spirit came into my life to teach me how to live and receive a better life.

Jesus' words in Matthew 11:28–30 captivated me, coinciding with the understanding forming in my life: "'Come to me, all you who are weary and burdened, and I will give you rest. Take my yoke upon you and learn from me, for I am gentle and humble in heart, and you will find rest for your souls. For my yoke is easy and my burden is light.'" A yoke has a connotation of working side by side with the same purpose. Since Jesus Christ knows more about God's desire or will than any other being, it behooves us to learn from Him.

The billboard event started me searching God's Word. My life began changing, slowly at first, but steadily. My outlook on life was definitively different. I came to the conclusion that it was God's plan for me to have a good life, a degree of success (3 John 2: "Beloved, I wish above all things that you may prosper and be in health, even as your soul prospers"). Why do I stress "degree of success"? Because success in life comes as the result of training, dedication, and pursuing the calling for which I am best suited.

Previously, I believed a close walk with Jesus Christ necessarily involved total separation from any recreation, even clean recreation. This concept made living for God almost impossible (unless, of course, I was a monk, which I certainly was not). After learning more about God I found that He wanted us to enjoy ourselves. Life held an air of excitement for me when I discovered the truth about God's Word.

Matthew 6:33 became my flagship scripture and has held sway

over my thinking. It was the map that has kept me focused on the direction for my life. My first responsibility was to keep my life centered in Jesus Christ and to search the scriptures for God's righteousness. I had confidence that God would lead me into a successful life (1 John 3:21; Hebrews 10:35), and He has not disappointed me.

The Holy Spirit taught me that I must have faith in God and be confident that I'm doing what God wants me to do. I must live in obedience to His Word. It was extremely important for me to base my trust in God. The foundation God wanted me to have did not rest on my parents' faith per se, or on what my church taught me, although it was good teaching. My faith must be mine *personally*. It had to come from God's Word and the revelations of the Holy Spirit.

Depending upon teaching from some person or persons may lead us erroneously. Sometimes people's views change. Teachers' views on God's Word may change. People sometimes may change their beliefs, but God's Word will not change. The Holy Spirit prompted me to understand that it was extremely important for me to determine what God meant when He inspired a writer to record His Word. God made such an impression on me that I want to emphatically relay the message to you, the reader.

Faith in God's Word had to be embedded in my soul. My faith must not be my mother's faith or my pastor's. My faith in God and His Word must be mine personally. I am reiterating this statement for a purpose. It's important that each child of God take this lesson to heart.

There is a saying worth repeating: "God has no grandchildren." Too many Christian folks depend on other people for answers from God. We should appreciate Godly associates, but our relationship with our Father is personal.

The day Jesus Christ entered my life was the day the Holy Spirit, the third person of the Godhead, took up residency within me and made His home in my life. Wherever I am, He is there; whatever I do, He is with me. How can I be sure of that? Because God's Word says He is with me. I have confidence in God's Word. People who truly trust God for their lives believe that the Bible is God's Word. They believe God speaks to them personally through scripture.

Nonbelievers consider it naive and foolish to place so much emphasis on the Bible. They argue that the Bible is filled with inaccuracies and is only a historical document. What they fail to realize is that the Bible is a supernatural book requiring faith to believe and understand. Jesus Christ confronted Nicodemus with this truth (John 3:3–21). When people try to understand the Bible by reading it like a novel or a history book, the understanding isn't there. It requires a born-again experience from the Holy Spirit to have insight into God's Word.

It is true that the Bible is a great source of history, and some passages were written for a different time, but the message is the same today as it was in days gone by. It was written for our learning, to impart to us patience, comfort, and hope (Romans 15:4), to bring us to an understanding of God and His nature.

God spoke His Word to us here on earth. If we are going to please God and receive blessings from Him, then we must have faith in God's Word and believe that He is speaking to each of us personally. Many folks do not feel close to God because they do not believe they qualify for God's favor. They think their lives are not good enough to have God's blessings. That is an erroneous concept that Satan has propagated in the minds of some people. The enemy is a liar, and he uses his lies to keep anyone from trusting God.

I encourage reading the third chapter of Colossians, paying special attention to those whom the text addressed. It appears that all God's Children come under the umbrella of this admonition. Slavery was a fact of life when Paul wrote his epistle, and yet slaves qualified for God's blessing right along with all others. God is not a respecter of persons (Colossians 3:25: "Anyone who does wrong will be repaid for his wrong, and there is no favoritism"). We should be grateful that God made each of us equal in His sight. We are all on a level playing field with our heavenly Father. The gift of Jesus Christ made all this possible. How blessed we are to have Christ in our lives.

The Word of God is talking to all of us equally. What He says to me, He says to you. However, God requires that each of us be obedient in whatever He requires of us. We all have different gifts that we are responsible for, and we are answerable to God for the use of those gifts.

It would be well to emphasize that God wants each of us to be individuals, not carbon copies of other folks. Sometimes we observe traits in others that we admire, but if we try to duplicate their ministry we shall fail in God's plan for our lives (Galatians 6:4–5: "Each one should test his own actions. Then he can take pride in himself, without comparing himself to somebody else, for each one should carry his own load"). God wants each of us to be precisely who He designed us to be. If you are trying to be someone else, then you are headed for failure. You are an individual—with individual qualities. Let those distinct characteristics make a way for you.

We should develop this thought further. If we could take an honest survey of all Christian people, we would probably find that most are defeated in their walk with God because they are comparing their walk with someone else's. They fail in the comparison. Therefore they think God is comparing them, too.

Until I truly learned that my relationship to Jesus Christ did not have to come up to someone else's standard, I was a second-class citizen to God. What a sense of relief and freedom came to me when I fully realized I was an individual and responsible for being what God created me to be (Galatians 6:4–5).

In the next chapter we shall look into the traits and characteristics that form our lives. After I accepted Christ as my savior and the Holy Spirit began the process of sanctification (changing the flaws in my character), the reason I was such a failure in life became increasingly clear.

I trust the following thoughts will be of help in your search for an abundant life in God. Matthew 6:33 promises a life in which God provides for us. When God is responsible for the outcome of our lives, the future seems secure.

(CHAPTER SEVEN)

Human Traits

> According as His divine power hath given unto us all things that pertain unto life and godliness through the knowledge of Him that hath called us to glory and virtue, by which are given unto us exceedingly great and precious promises, that by these ye might be partakers of the divine nature, having escaped the corruption that is in the world through lust. (2 PETER 1:3–4)

In the beginning humanity was endowed with God's nature, but after the fall in the Garden these characteristics became lustful and evil. All of us share some traits, but some characteristics are more predominant than others. Folks will display destructive mannerisms that others cannot understand. Why do they allow such natures to control their lives? If I examine my life I may have peculiarities that are as bad or even worse (Luke 6:41: "'Why do you look at the speck of sawdust in your brother's eye and pay no attention to the plank in your own eye?'").

Most qualities were placed in us by God. He made us to be peaceful, successful, and wise—to have an abundant life. We were made in the image of God (Genesis 1:26). Satan entered the picture and perverted all those beautiful traits. They became destructive, rather than productive.

In this chapter we examine a few traits to see how they were perverted. It is God's desire to restore Godly characteristics. We can have a nature that will produce a life of abundance.

That is what this book is about. The Holy Spirit will guide each of us into correcting habits and traits that destroy our chance for a copious life (John 10:10). Observing each trait, we can see a counterpart. Habits and traits are extremely difficult to change. Many times we repeat the same destructive decisions because of a flawed quality.

We will discuss here some characteristics that can have a bearing on our quality of life; some are God given, others are earned. Our environment, from childhood, plays a major role in the development of our outlook on life. Some traits emerge while we are growing up. Being raised in a Christian home has great benefit, but some natures are contrary to having an abundant existence.

PATIENCE

Patience is not an inborn trait. It is a learned quality, as is trust, a characteristic the Holy Spirit teaches us through experiences (James 1–4). The desire for instant gratification is part of humanity's failure and seems to grow worse with each generation.

Lack of patience was one of the sins contributing to my failure. Gambling comes from a desire to have money instantly, without earning it. Gambling was vice I acquired in the army, and the Holy Spirit zeroed in on that sin. The Word of God condemns quick gain as a destructive sin (1 Timothy 6:9: "People who want to get rich fall into temptation and a trap and into many foolish and harmful desires that plunge men into ruin and destruction"). Often we think the Holy Spirit is only interested in sins that damn our souls from living eternally with God, but God is interested in correcting sins that destroy our chances of having a victorious life in the here and now.

The desire to have money quickly, especially without working for it, is the desire to circumvent a learning process. It would be easy for God to provide money to each Christian. In fact, He will pave the streets with gold in eternity (Revelation 21:21: "The great street of the city was of pure gold, like transparent glass"). We shall walk on it like we do blacktop down here. Why is money so hard to come by here on earth? Why doesn't God make it easy for His Children to have money?

It's a learning process. The Bible addresses money (mammon), teaching us that we should not place undue value on it. We cannot serve money and God at the same time (Matthew 6:24: "'No one can serve two masters. Either he will hate the one and love the other, or he will be devoted to the one and despise the other. You cannot serve both God and money'"). It is well documented that people who win the lottery are broke and in debt within a reasonably short time. Andrew Carnegie, the steel magnate of days gone by, tried to give away money to individuals to better their lives. Each time he did, their lives were destroyed. He decided to give money to libraries, thus giving anyone an opportunity to better themselves if they are willing to work for it. Generally speaking, if you can't earn it, you can't keep it.

The desire to have money quickly causes great harm to families, businesses, and churches. There is nothing wrong with having money. It is the love of money that is the sin. Love of money instigates all sorts of activities that impact lives negatively—gambling, cheating, stealing and other criminal acts (Timothy 6:10: "For the love of money is a root of all kinds of evil. Some people, eager for money, have wandered from the faith and pierced themselves with many griefs"). Because guidelines must be established, God placed Matthew 6:33 in His Word as a plan for us to follow.

Borrowing money or purchasing through debt has been the downfall of many businesses, marriages, churches, and individuals. Having debt is not wrong—in fact, it can be helpful—but it must be entered into wisely. Debit cards, credit cards, car loans, and the like are destructive unless they are handled carefully. Borrowing money pledges our future earnings, many times beyond our earning ability. I have known Christian folks who went into debt and their future looked bleak. They began to pray for Jesus to return and take them out of their dilemma. What an ungodly view of God's Word.

Borrowed money can destroy our chances of getting ahead in life. Borrowed money enhances income for banks and lending institutions. We become slaves to their programs. Until we are free of debt, there is very little chance of getting ahead in life. Instant gratification encourages debt.

Isn't it amazing how much God's Word teaches about having a good life? In my early days I thought God's Word was solely concerned with my relationship with Jesus Christ—with whether I went to heaven or hell. I really did not know God was interested in an abundant life for me here and now (John 10:10).

Having patience is a product of Godly wisdom from the Holy Spirit. We possess our soul (our emotions, our desires, and our will) in our patience (Luke 21:19: "'In your patience possess ye your souls'"; King James Version). Elements that make up our soul are controlled by our patience. *Soul* and *heart* are sometimes synonymous in God's Word, referring to the very seat of our life. When our heart and soul are under the control of patience, we shall prosper—even our health prospers (3 John 2; Proverbs 3:20–27).

Many times we borrow money to buy something we could get along without, until we had the money. We should at least have a well-thought-out plan. Generally, we want what we want immediately; our emotions are in control. The neighbor has one, so we want one (we have to "keep up with the Joneses"). The Bible calls it emulation—jealousy, covetousness (Luke 12:15: "Then Jesus said to them, 'Watch out! Be on your guard against all kinds of greed; a man's life does not consist in the abundance of his possessions'").

Patience is a product of experience, of the hard knocks of life—experiences that teach discipline. Patience is a valuable quality in a person, yet it is difficult to acquire. Society and human nature work against patience and discipline. This could be why God has so much to say about patience and discipline.

To paraphrase Jesus, good, honest, productive people bring forth fruit with their patience. He is talking about being successful. There are many metaphors in the Word of God, and we all know that Jesus uses illustrations and parables to reveal many truths (Luke 8:11–15). This parable talks about putting seed into the ground and if the soil is good and patience is applied, then a harvest is sure to come.

We are justified by faith in Jesus Christ. Therefore, we have peace with our Father (God). We have access to God and His benefits. We endure tribulations, knowing that tribulations nurture patience. We go through difficult times, and the experience causes hope (Romans 5:1–4). Paul is saying that a child of God has access to God's benefits in everyday life. We are going to have difficulties in life, but we know those problems will work to our advantage by producing patience and hope. Difficulties work to our good when we are in Christ Jesus, but it requires patience to reap the benefits (Romans 8:28).

Faith plays a crucial role in our lives. We will talk more about faith later, but for now, I want to comment on faith interacting with patience. James 1:3 tells us that God will test our faith, compelling us to wait for an answer, to see if we are going to trust Him: "Because you know that the testing of your faith develops perseverance."

Faith that is successfully tested is more valuable than gold or silver (1 Peter 1:6–7). The writer is using the analogy of gold and silver to represent something important to us. If we are going to trust God and have faith that our request will be answered, then patience must be involved. We need to lay hold of this truth because our next request to God may depend upon understanding it (Hebrews 10:35–36). Many people have given up on God answering their request, just before receiving an answer (Isaiah 40:31; Galatians 6:7–9).

It is surprising to learn how much the Bible has to say about patience (cf. Hebrews 10:35–36; 2 Peter 1:2–9, to name just two passages). It would be rewarding to do a thorough search for everything in the Bible pertaining to patience. Patience is an important skill for the Holy Spirit to teach us because of the time element we discussed in chapter 4. Humanity wants everything right away.

Technology is adding to our urge toward instant gratification. Microwave ovens, computers, instant messaging, faster transportation, nonstop music, instant meals, to name just a few things, are encouraging us to demand everything without waiting. Patience is a fast-disappearing quality, and the Bible is warning us of the consequences.

Christians, too, are becoming impatient with God. He doesn't answer prayers quickly enough; He makes us wait for the resolution of situations that irritate us. With all our technology we feel that God is too slow for our generation. We must remember that patience is learned by waiting for time to pass before receiving something. Waiting goes against our grain today.

A well-known, respected scientist taught in his seminars that science had developed to the point that God was too slow to meet today's fast pace. He said: "We can go to the moon, produce life in test tubes, and clone life. We can do anything God can do, but we can do it sooner. We can get along without God."

About that time a voice from the sky said, "Would you like to have a contest?"

The scientist asked, "Is that you, God?"

"Yes it is," said God.

The scientist encouraged his class to follow him to an open field, where he planned to create an image by using soil and a special formula. Everything was set up and the time frame established. The scientist had figured into his equation a scientific method that circumvented time. Natural laws required time to develop the image. With the scientist's formula it could be done almost instantly.

The scientist asked God, "Are you ready?" The scientist picked up some dirt to begin his experiment.

God said, "You must not use that dirt. I made that dirt. Make your own dirt."

We humans cannot create, however. All we can do is rearrange what God has created.

PROCRASTINATION AND LACK OF DISCIPLINE

Procrastination was a success-destroying sin in my early life. When I was in the army an officer called my attention to the tendency to procrastinate in my psychological makeup. After I was discharged from the service I found a job in a car dealership. I was hired to detail used cars for sale. The owner called attention to my flaw—procrastination.

After working for the agency awhile, I thought I was doing a bang-up job, but Mr. Simon, the owner, was not pleased with my work.

He said: "Jordan, you're good at cleaning up these vehicles, but you're the worst procrastinator I ever saw. You do the big things, but you waste too much time getting to the details—the small things. If you don't break that habit I'll let you go."

I retorted, "If that's the way you feel, I'll quit."

I quit a good job. My temper and pride refused to accept correction. This combination was destructive to my military life; it was destructive in everything I tried to do. No doubt, this nature was strongly responsible for my rebelling against God. The Holy Spirit allowed me to sink low enough in life that I was willing to pay attention—to the billboard.

Although this chapter is not about pride, I feel it necessary to address the subject before continuing with procrastination. False pride is the basis for the problems of humankind. False pride was a dominating factor in Lucifer's downfall. We, therefore, have the same disease. The Word of God is filled with admonition against false pride (Proverbs 16:18: "Pride goes before destruction, a haughty spirit before a fall").

Pride keeps us from listening to advice and warnings. That was my dilemma. Until I reached rock bottom in my self-worth, I refused advice. After my conversion, the Holy Spirit started a sanctification process, and I began finding out what the Word of God had to say about my pressing problem of pride (Proverbs 16:18; 29:23). I asked God to help me overcome my problem and listen to folks who wanted to help me. God focused my attention on what others had tried to tell me. Procrastination and a lack of discipline were ruining my life. Those two flaws travel hand in hand.

Putting things off until later is a costly habit. It allows things to pile up until they become big problems. The accumulation of small, unattended-to matters will eventually undermine the success of any project. I was putting off responsibilities that I dreaded or disliked, telling myself I would do them later, but "later" never came. I am grateful to the Holy Spirit for pointing out to me that procrastination and lack of discipline were debilitating sins in my life. Those two sins could have damned my soul for eternity. Hell will be occupied by folks who had good intentions but put off seeking Jesus Christ until a more convenient time (Hebrews 3:7–15).

The supernatural hand of God is undetected by human beings because He acts in ways that are natural. We are natural, physical beings, but there are things in our lives that are not natural, although they are common to us, things such as the subconscious mind, thought patterns, intuition, fear, joy, peace, faith, and our souls. We take all these things for granted because they are common to everyday activity, but they are supernatural. They are gifts from a supernatural God.

Consider the following questions:

- How many times have we allowed our emotions to destroy our chances of succeeding?
- How many times have we destroyed our financial success and even our marriages by acting on sinful secret desires?
- How many times has our strong will turned out to lead us in the wrong direction?

Determining God's thinking on any project is the sure way to success—it is part of seeking God's righteousness.

Jesus Christ promised me a better life, and now He is correcting things that have hindered my success. I emphasize this fact: God was pointing out my faults to me. The Holy Spirit was encouraging me to make changes, helping me with my infirmities (Romans 8:26: "Likewise, the Spirit also helpeth our infirmity"; King James Version).

When I reminisce about the business God directed me into, I can see the reason for it being insurance sales. God's divine wisdom knew I would have to canvass houses and farms if I was going to succeed. God could have chosen any business He desired for me, but He chose one that required tremendous discipline and in which there was no room for procrastination (my two worst flaws).

Soliciting was my only means of finding prospects. I learned from experience that if I canvassed, I would find interested parties. Sales resulted. I thoroughly disliked this method of finding prospects. I wanted to be in a business that had folks coming to me. Then I wouldn't have to knock on some stranger's door. God didn't make it easy for me—I was forced into facing my faults.

When I considered not soliciting and yielded to procrastination, I remembered the billboard and the promise God made to me. The Holy Spirit brought me face-to-face with my flaws. I would talk to the Lord and return to canvassing.

One cold, snowy morning, I really dreaded going out to canvass, but I had to make fifty dollars to pay rent and buy groceries. (It doesn't sound like much, but at the time, it was equivalent to working a week on a job.) I forced myself to knock on doors, and that day I made three times what I needed—more than enough to meet my family's needs. God continually proved to me that if I would defeat the success-destroying inadequacy in my makeup, I could expect an abundant life.

The battle with discipline and procrastination went on for nearly a year, becoming less severe as the year progressed. I noticed that other things in my life were changing, such as reading the Bible and praying. I seemed to have more energy, my eating habits changed. My self-worth was rising. When I looked into the mirror I liked what I saw. My old nature was changing right in front of my eyes.

Moreover, I found it much easier talking to strangers. I could think on my feet and make a convincing presentation. Little did I know that God was training me for a ministry. Jesus Christ's plan for our lives goes far beyond what we observe in the present. He is working things out for our future (Jeremiah 29:11: "'For I know the plans I have for you,' declares the Lord").

Over the next twenty years I hired 250 men to sell insurance for my agency. Out of those 250 men, only fifteen really made it in sales. Many had a true gift for sales, but they couldn't discipline themselves to canvass. Procrastination got the better of them. They found things more to their liking to occupy their time, things like drinking coffee, staying at home, loafing rather than canvassing. You can imagine the numerous excuses I heard over a twenty-year period. God was allowing me to see firsthand how many people are affected by the demons of procrastination and lack of discipline.

I am convinced that any average person can have a degree of success, if he or she can overcome procrastination and gain discipline. Failure in business and ministry will generally come from those two killers; many of us fight them all our lives. Procrastination and lack of discipline lurk in the shadows of many lives, ready to destroy if allowed to surface.

I want to relate an event that underscores the Holy Spirit's work in my life. I was staying away from home in a motel, canvassing the town. One morning it looked like rain and I didn't feel well (not really sick, just lazy). I decided to stay in the room instead of working. Procrastination was pushing hard that morning, and lack of discipline was winning.

The Holy Spirit reminded me: "Sam, do you remember the army captain telling you that excuses will not make car payments, house payments, or help you succeed in the army? Excuses won't get the job done. Successful people work and succeed in spite of all odds. Do you remember the dealership and the conversation with Mr. Simon? Now, you must get up and do your work. Get yourself by the necktie and force yourself out that door."

I dressed and went out to canvass. I made a week's wages that day in sales. It sounds too natural to be God, but God is supernaturally natural. I am talking about breaking the demons in my nature that kept me from having a good life. Whatever your success-destroying habit, God will help you overcome it. It won't be easy, but it'll be worth the effort. These problems have been around since the beginning of time, and God wants us to be aware of the destruction they cause (Proverbs 26:13: "The slothful man saith, 'There is a lion in the way; a lion is in the streets'"; King James Version).

INNER MOTIVATION

We hear much about self-motivation. It's important to be able to motivate ourselves. It's one of the secrets to success. Many people have very little self-motivation. They are motivated by someone telling them what to do, when to do it, and how to do it—they require a boss. The business community works on a boss–labor system. There is little chance for advancement, except perhaps to aspire to a boss's position. The system works because many people need someone supervising them. There is nothing wrong with working in this system—the wrong is in needing someone to keep us motivated.

Many people shirk responsibility when the boss is not watching. If they were not required to keep certain hours, they would either be late or not show up at all. Folks who have this problem should know that it is not the way God wants His people to operate.

There may be nothing wrong with our job, and we should be thankful we have one. The wrong is in our lack of inner motivation. A Spirit-filled child of God should be the best worker on any job. Our motivation should not be money; rather, it should be to complete our projects well and receive money for doing the job. It sounds confusing at first, but it is all in the way we view our work. Workers who watch the clock, waiting for quitting time and payday, won't get a raise or be considered for promotions. God's people should be motivated to give 110 percent to their work.

You can be assured that sooner or later supervisors will notice those who give more than is asked of a worker. When motivated by the Holy Spirit, we are givers, not takers. Over a period of time the Holy Spirit–filled employee will be elevated to a leadership position. Holy Spirit–motivated people are not slackers, they are leaders (Deuteronomy 28:13: "The Lord will make you the head, not the tail. If you pay attention to the commands of the Lord your God that I give you this day and carefully follow them, you will always be at the top, never at the bottom"). God promises a good life, if we put His kingdom first and seek His righteousness. Doing things God's way will certainly be different from doing them the world's way.

DOUBLE MINDEDNESS

Cognitive dissonance is a term used by psychologists to describe what James 1:8 calls double-minded. It means a confused mental condition resulting from simultaneously holding incongruous, often mutually contradicting beliefs. In simpler terms it means trying to live both sides of a belief. Many folks try to have a life in Christ, but they live inconsistently with the Word of God. Both psychologists and the Bible declare these folks to be double-minded: if the condition persists, they are unstable in all their ways; active faith is not possible, and a God-inspired life escapes them (James 1:6–8).

The Bible is filled with accounts of men and women who lived with God's blessings—people like Abraham, Joshua, David, Sarah. Those writings are for our learning, comfort, patience, and hope (Romans 15:4). Faith in God's Word will bring a life of success. We can let our full weight down on God and rest assured of God's favor (Psalm 1:2–3).

The crux of the whole matter depends upon having faith in God's Word. If a person truly accepts that God's Word means what He is saying and is addressed to us personally, we are placed in a position of expectation (Hebrews 11:6). Some folks do not really believe God exists or they think that if He does exist, He isn't interested in their personal affairs. The Word declares that God is very much interested in our personal lives and that He rewards faith.

If we have genuine, active faith in God, that He really does exist, and that He will reward anyone diligently seeking His will, then we have a confidence that propels us toward success in life (Matthew 6:33; Proverbs 3:1–10; Psalm 37:3–5) Having faith and living a life in God indicates a supernatural mind-set (John 3:1–3). Some people attend church and profess being children of God, but they do not have faith that God's Word means what it says—to them it is a book of history or religion. They do not understand that God's Word is filled with life-related promises. It's not a book of superstitions that brings good fortune when we rub it, like a rabbit's foot. Having faith in God's Word is a way of life—a life of trust in God, whether He gives us what we want or not (Habakkuk 3:17–19). We belong to Him; we are sheep in His pasture (Psalm 100:3).

Being a child of God is such a privilege. In Jesus Christ, God provided a bridge for us to come to Him. Before Jesus Christ came and redeemed us from our lost position, we had no access to God. It was through God's love and kindness that He made a way for us. It would be egotistical for anyone to allow his or her trust and faith in God to be measured by the degree to which He answers prayers. God does answer prayer, but our love for Him should be steadfast even if He seems never to grant another request (Habakkuk 3:17–19).

I have included the preceding paragraph for the sake of those who have lost faith in God because of unanswered petitions. This attitude has been around for millennia. The heart of God is saddened by such astigmatic thinking (Malachi 3:13–14: "'You have said harsh things against me,' says the Lord. 'Yet you ask, "What have we said against you?"' You have said, "It is futile to serve God. What did we gain by carrying out his requirements and going about like mourners before the Lord Almighty?"'").

In the next chapter we will explore the subject of money and possessions. They are in constant competition for first place with Jesus Christ. We do not want to admit this fact, but we must face the truth. Jesus addresses this matter in the sixth chapter of Matthew (verses 19–24). Money plays a vital role in all our lives.

God is not opposed to money per se; it is the love of money that is the problem (1 Timothy 6:9–10). *Love* is a term used often in God's Word to measure its place: we shall love one and hate the other. In all honesty, we place an extremely high value on possessions.

The Matthew 6:33 principle places money and possessions last.

(CHAPTER EIGHT)

The Subject of Money and Success

> No man can serve two masters; for he will hate the one and love the other; or else he will hold to the one and despise the other. Ye cannot serve God and money. (MATTHEW 6:24)

Money and possessions are important to almost everyone and instigate major questions concerning our relationship to God. We have God's promise that He will supply our needs, and yet our requests go unanswered so many times. Why is it difficult to receive an answer from God concerning money?

Perhaps an answer to this question lies in the fact that God cannot always trust us with money (Psalm 39:6: "Man is a mere phantom as he goes to and fro: He bustles about, but only in vain; he heaps up wealth, not knowing who will get it"). It seems that when our character has developed to a certain level, God does bless us with more abundance. When we seek God and His righteousness first, material things are added to us (Matthew 6:33). God increases our lives so that we can be better witnesses for the kingdom of God. We make better witnesses for Christ when we have abundance and our lives are productive. There are, of course, exceptions to this general observation.

God gives us considerable leeway in making decisions. When we make decisions contrary to God's purpose, we are on our own; success or failure depends on our ability and luck, and that is not a very stable situation. When we make decisions according to God's Word, God becomes responsible for us (1 John 5:14–15). We are sheep in His pasture (Psalm 100:3), which *is* a stable situation.

God gives us power to obtain wealth so that we can fulfill His purpose "to establish His covenant on earth" (Deuteronomy 8:17–18). It's enlightening to read in the New Testament that God warns against being carried away with the desire for money. It's important to understand how God feels toward the subject of possessions and money. The Bible doesn't support the belief that God is displeased with His Children having wealth. Abraham (one of God's chosen servants) was wealthy. Abraham loved God and spent his life in His service. Abraham was a man of faith, a true faith in God, and we see no evidence of God's frowning on Abraham's possessions. God is not against money and possessions; God is against the love of money for its own sake (1 Timothy 6:5-19). Wealth tends to foster an attitude of power and superiority. God is then placed in a subordinate position, a position He will not tolerate.

God's Word spends considerable time on the subject of wealth, because it dominates so much of our lives. Jesus said that it is easier for a camel to go through the eye of a needle than for a rich man to enter the kingdom of God (Matthew 19:23–24). When His disciples heard Him make that statement they were amazed and perplexed. After all, everyone desires to be successful in life. Does Jesus' statement mean that we desire something that will keep us out of the kingdom of God? Jesus answers that question (verse 26): "With men it is impossible, but with God all things are possible."

Peter shows his concern for himself and the other disciples: "We left our fishing business to follow you, what will be our reward?" Peter and the others had walked away from their boats. They were human and desired financial security, as we all do (verse 27).

At this point Jesus strikes at the heart of the Matthew 6:33

principle. He declares that anyone who puts God's kingdom first shall receive one hundred times more than what has been given up, plus eternal life. In essence, He is saying that a child of God must set the right priorities in life, if he or she wants God's favor (Matthew 19:28–29). This position begs an important question, a question that plagued me when I was introduced to Matthew 6:33 on the billboard: if I turned my life over to Christ and put God's kingdom first, could I expect God to provide for my and my family's needs? What does God's Word teach on this conspicuous subject?

I have introduced numerous passages affirming that God will bless anyone who puts His kingdom first and obeys His commands (i.e., anyone who follows His Word under the leadership of the Holy Spirit). Deuteronomy 8:18, Psalms 1:2–3 and 37:3–4, Proverbs 3:1–10, Malachi 3:10–11, Matthew 6:33, Luke 6:38, and 3 John 2 all pertain to material blessings.

After studying these passages, it would be preposterous to doubt that God is involved with fulfilling our financial needs and even our desires. But what about the question of whether we can expect God to make us wealthy?

A straightforward answer to that question is problematic and complex. Wealth is enigmatic and has numerous, conflicting meanings for different people. *Opulence* may be a better word, because it implies comfort. Different things make people comfortable; a variety of natures is found in humanity. Some require material possessions; others are more content with virtue; still others desire wisdom and knowledge. The list could be extensive. There's one common denominator, however: there must be an abundance of whatever desired, and there must be enough financial wherewithal to meet the requirements. Jesus Christ paid the price to meet that need (John 10:10).

Success, too, has many connotations. If you asked the missionary in Africa for his or her definition of prosperity, it would be quite different from that of the head of a large corporation. Before Jesus Christ entered my life I had an erroneous slant on attainment. I thought that God was against my having wealth, but when achievement is properly understood we see that it is God's good pleasure for His children to prosper (3 John 2). From the beginning of time God wanted human beings to succeed in bringing the world under submission; God intended for us to fulfill the command of Genesis 1:27–28: "Be fruitful and increase in number; fill the earth and subdue it. Rule . . ."

God created our character and desires for a good life. Satan perverted those qualities into destructive, self-centered desires. It is God's plan to restore to us a Godly nature (2 Peter 1:3–10)—not restored to perfection (that shall come in our resurrected bodies; 1 Corinthians 15:49–57). But it is God's plan to restore enough of our character to have a good life on earth (Psalm 1:2–3; Matthew 6:33; James 1:22–25).

The children of God should hold God's interests above their own. Each of us who has an income is clearly directed to support the kingdom of God through tithing and offerings (Luke 6:38). It is our privilege and duty to support God's kingdom with a portion of our income.

In private counseling sessions concerning financial hardship, more often than not, I discovered a lack of adhering to God's Word on the subject of tithing and offerings. Reading Malachi 3:7–11 will motivate us to give God His portion. We cannot expect Him to bless us financially unless we obey His commands. If we follow God's method of dealing with prosperity He will honor His Word. Too many times we attempt to circumvent His Word, thinking we can beat the odds; we are only fooling ourselves (Galatians 6:7–9).

The first thing I learned about God's promises is that prosperity does not come out of the blue, like winning the lottery; it comes through a process. Success is not determined by the size of one's bank account. Generally speaking, money will be involved, but success is much greater than financial wealth. Mr. Johnson, the restaurant and motel pioneer, defined success as "a proper pursuit of a worthwhile ambition." That's a good definition.

The billboard exhortation promised me a better life if I prioritized my life. I had to learn some hard lessons to receive the promise. Seeking God's kingdom was the first requirement. I did that right away, or at least started doing it.

The idea of seeking His righteousness was more difficult for me to understand. That seemed to have a connotation of doing things right—God's way. I had habits and flaws that had to be changed if I was going to be recipient of an abundant life. Restoration begins with accepting Jesus Christ as our redeemer. The Word of God must be our instruction book (Psalm 119:105: "Your word is a lamp to my feet and a light for my path"). The Holy Spirit helps us understand the Word and empowers us to live in accordance with it.

This chapter looks at characteristics and desires that have been perverted but that God wants to restore. Sin came into our lives in the Garden and separated us from God and His promises. One literal translation of the word *sin* means to miss the mark (analogous to shooting at and missing a target). Sin in our life will shut off our access to God.

There are sins pertaining to anything we attempt, for example:

- Sins against marriage: being unkind to our spouse, being unfaithful.
- Sins against financial success: being lazy, being undependable, stealing, procrastinating, being untruthful, refusing instruction.

God wants to remedy those transgressions that keep us from having a life of abundance. Many times, we don't want to hear what God's Word says about eradicating debilitating situations. We would rather God bring our ship in, without our help—by a miracle.

After I received Jesus Christ into my life, the Holy Spirit began working on destructive sins that were keeping me down. I had to be taught. All the instructions are in God's Word, but we often view the Bible as a religious book, instead of an instruction manual for life. I'm still learning after fifty years. We never exhaust all there is to know about God in this lifetime. The more I learn about God, the closer my relationship with Him becomes.

Learning about myself, my flaws and habits that are unacceptable in light of God's Word, was difficult for me. I learned that God was not angry with me because of these flaws. The Holy Spirit was teaching me to face up to my failures. Some of my failures were deleted with help from the Holy Spirit and God's Word; others I still have. It's a lifelong pursuit. We are human. We are not, nor will we ever be, perfect in this life—just forgiven.

It's interesting to note, when reading the Old Testament, how often the children of Israel turned away from God to serve false idols that were unable to deliver answers to prayers. Israel continued making that mistake. You'd think the people would have realized how costly it was to make such errors. But do we not do the very same thing when we try to circumvent or evade God's Word, hoping He won't see us, or thinking that maybe we can get away with it this time?

Today we don't build temples for idols or dedicate groves to honor various gods, but the principles are the same. There's only one true God, and money is not worthy of our focus for trusting. Therefore, God admonishes us to establish priorities: Seek first the kingdom of God and His righteousness, and God will see to it that our needs are met.

In our next chapter we shall differentiate between the kingdom of heaven and the kingdom of God. In most instances they appear to be the same, but by careful textual analysis we can detect the distinction. Understanding the separation helps us see our role in seeking first the kingdom of God.

At first glance the difference appears to be moot, but a clear picture may help us understand some unpleasant occurrences in the work of God. In seeking first the kingdom of God we need all the understanding we can obtain. We can be assured we will encounter obstacles. The Devil is determined that we not find the way, for it will bring us into an abundant life and the kingdom of God shall prosper.

(CHAPTER NINE)

The Kingdom of God in Contradistinction to the Kingdom of Heaven

Prioritizing my life was the first thing the Holy Spirit required of me: Seek the kingdom of God. Accepting Christ into my life was primary. I couldn't learn any more until I was born into the kingdom of God (John 3:3: "Jesus declared, 'I tell you the truth, no one can see the kingdom of God unless he is born again'"). For a few years after accepting Christ I thought God's promises of a better life were strictly for my benefit; I did not realize what seeking His kingdom really meant. I was in such bad shape personally that the Holy Spirit allowed me to think that way for a while.

I bunched all of Matthew 6:33 into two meanings. First, if I accepted Jesus Christ, I would have God's righteousness. Second, I would have God's blessings in the form of material things.

The time came for me to learn the next step. God was going to lead me into a much deeper understanding of what it meant to seek His kingdom.

Searching scriptures on the kingdom of God led me to find another phrase—the kingdom of heaven. On the surface the concepts seemed to be synonymous, but with further study I found they were different.

Distinguishing the difference helped me to understand the Bible and to learn my role in seeking first the kingdom of God. Defining the difference helped me understand cantankerous folks in a church body. They do exist (which I can affirm from my years as a pastor). Expectations are elevated to unreasonable levels in church communities. There are antagonists as well as protagonists in a church body.

Seeking first the kingdom of God calls for considerable thought. Unless we have clarity on what we are seeking, confusion and excessive piety (a form of church-bred religious fervor) may be the result. The kingdom of God and the kingdom of heaven are referred to many times in the Bible. To understand the difference we must pay close attention to the contexts in which they are mentioned. Wherever the kingdom of God is expressed it refers to the genuine article, without flaw and without being observable, such as is found in the heart of an individual enjoying a new birth by the Holy Spirit, those who are "born again" (John 3:3, 5). It is a truly spiritual kingdom.

An interesting discourse on this subject is found in Luke 17:20–21. Jesus is talking to unbelieving Pharisees. The Pharisees wanted to see the kingdom of God on earth—its physical manifestation. Jesus is referring to Himself when He says that the kingdom of God is in your midst, or within (as the King James version has it). Jesus Christ says it does not come by observation—physically. It comes through a spiritual birth at this time. The physical kingdom of God shall come during the thousand-year reign, in fulfillment of the Davidic covenant (2 Samuel 7:16: "Your house and your kingdom will endure forever before me; your throne will be established forever").

Until the thousand-year reign, the kingdom of God is in the hearts of "born-again" Christians. This is the reason Jesus answered Pilate the way He did when he stated, "My kingdom is not of this world" (John 18:35–36).

Now, we introduce the kingdom of heaven—the physical, organized church, the community with which we gather for worship with all its traditions and religious ceremonies. Jesus calls our attention to seven parables concerning the "mysteries of the kingdom of heaven" (Matthew 13). As we read the first nine verses of chapter 13 we are given a clear picture of the organized church and its struggles. It's obvious that not everyone who came under the influence of the church embraced His teachings, at least for very long.

Jesus begins by making it clear that members of the organized church are the sowers of the seed (that is, the Word of God). He also makes it clear that the soil is the heart (soul) of an individual, in which the seed is sown.

Four types of hearts (souls) are illustrated in this discourse. They represent conditions found in people who come under the influence of the Gospel. If we are honest with ourselves, we can identify where we fit in the picture.

In verse 4, the seed falls where it cannot grow and is devoured by birds (i.e., the person is not prepared to receive and does not act on the Word).

In verses 5–6, the soil accepts the seed but it is a superficial experience, without the desire to go deeper. When unpleasant conditions prevail, growth withers away.

In verse 7, thorns (the deceitfulness of riches and cares of life) render the seed ineffective.

In verse 8, the seed falls on good soil and brings forth fruit, some a hundredfold, some sixty, and some thirty.

In verse 9, Jesus injects a thought that requires insight: He refers to the inner ear of the soul. If there is a hunger or desire, then understanding of these parables will bring revelation.

My favorite text on this particular parable is Mark 4:13–24, in which Jesus essentially calls the parable of the sower the granddaddy of all parables when he states that if we do not understand this parable, we cannot grasp *any* parable.

The seven parables of Matthew 13, called by Jesus "the mysteries of the kingdom of heaven" (verse 11), depict the organized church during the present church age. Jesus uses metaphors to show there are good and bad elements in the church body.

The parable of the tares among the wheat (verses 24–30) vividly describes why problematic situations in a church must be handled carefully. Often, when human effort is exercised to remove or correct someone causing difficulty, a relative or close friend may be hurt.

Drawing our attention to the parable of the dragnet (verses 47–51), Jesus uses the illustration of a net that is cast into the sea and gathers every kind of fish, some good and some bad. He tells us that "at the end of the age . . . the angels will come forth" and "separate the wicked from among the just." This is a warning to us to be careful in judging and labeling people—Christian or not Christian. God alone makes that determination.

In studying these seven parables we understand why Jesus Christ wants us to seek first the kingdom of God (Matthew 6:33) rather than the kingdom of heaven. The kingdom of heaven is the sphere of Christian profession during the church age. It is a mingled body of truth and falsity, wheat and tares, worthy and unworthy. It is hampered by hypocrisy, formalism, competition, and worldliness. Yet with all this adulterated intermix, Jesus Christ sees the true children of the kingdom of God within the church body; there are flaws and faults in the earthly church, yet it is God's system for this age. It will be God's plan until the church is removed from the earth by way of the rapture (note that the word *rapture* is not found in the Bible; it refers to being snatched away or plucked up by force) (1 Thessalonians 4:13–18; 1 Corinthians 15:51–53).

A fellow minister and I were holding soul-winning seminars throughout the United States. In our work we detected a resistance in many churches and were hindered in our efforts by people who were against personally winning souls. We became discouraged and started castigating the organized church.

The Holy Spirit urged us to refrain from speaking against the church. It is true that the church has inadequacies, yet it is God's system for this age. He revealed to us that the church is the husk that protects the fruit (grain) until it has matured. The church serves many great and beneficial functions in the community and to winning the lost. The process of training and encouraging believers has been the church's responsibility. Removing the husk (the physical church) before God's time will destroy the fruit (Mark 4:26–29).

Numerous commentators have gone to great lengths to explain the difference between God's kingdom and the kingdom of heaven for the following reasons:

- Many folks have been hurt by activities in a church body and no longer attend church, raising a legitimate question: how could an all-powerful, loving God allow such things to occur in His church body? We see by our study that God does not want broken relationships, but they do happen. We should not stop attending church but instead use the situation to grow into maturity (Hebrews 10:25: "Let us not give up meeting together, as some are in the habit of doing, but let us encourage one another—and all the more as you see the Day approaching"). We must remember that Satan, our enemy, sometimes sows seeds of discord.
- Our priority must be the desire to see a soul saved and grow into maturity. The physical aspects (building, music, etc.) of a church body are tools to help accomplish God's work.
- The local church body represents Jesus Christ's vineyard. It is a place for us to be actively and regularly involved in building the kingdom of God.

A day will come when God will say to His Son, Jesus Christ, it is time to bring your church home. Christ will appear in the sky, and the Holy Spirit will usher the redeemed to meet Him in the air (both those who have died and those that are still alive). From that moment on, there will be a change in God's plan on earth (1 Corinthians 15:51–54; 2 Thessalonians 2:1–12, verse 7 of which tells us that "someone" will hinder until He is removed, or taken out of the way).

I believe that "someone" is the Holy Spirit, whose responsibility at the present time is to build and protect the church of the Lord Jesus Christ. The power of the Holy Spirit in the organized church is holding back a tide of evil.

There's considerable disagreement on the time element in these scriptures concerning "The Day of the Lord" versus the rapture of the church. The "Day of the Lord" probably refers to a time when Jesus returns to earth and sets up His millennial reign, which happens approximately seven years after the church is taken out.

The study of exact time elements goes beyond the scope of this book. Our basic concern here is to realize that it all will happen and that we need to be ready, whatever time it occurs. This world will not be a place to be when the church is taken out. Seeking first the kingdom of God includes efforts to reach as many folks with the gospel message as we possibly can, before Jesus Christ does come for His church.

It is important for all of us to remember that God loves His creation, especially humanity. He is not willing for any of us to perish. He wants all to come to a place of repentance (2 Peter 3:9). For this reason God is holding back closing the church age. God is counting on each of us to do what we can to help Him with His mission.

It is not easy for us to realize that God needs us (we are so locked in on Him helping us). We might understand why He needs us if we can comprehend that He is a spirit and His kingdom is spiritual. Since we are material or physical, we are better equipped to deal with material matters.

If we can grasp this concept, then we can understand why Jesus Christ had to come to earth as a baby boy. Then He grew into manhood and was filled with the Holy Spirit at His baptism (Mark 1:9–11). He then proceeded to do the work of God's kingdom on earth. To deal with physical matters, he had to be a physical person. We must also remember that He had to be filled with the Holy Spirit in order to do the work of the kingdom of God (Mark 1:10: "As Jesus was coming out of the water, he saw heaven being torn open and the Spirit descending on him like a dove").

Jesus' responsibility was to put the church into operation. He paid the supreme sacrifice to do that: the cup in the garden, the cross and resurrection. The church was born for the purpose of fulfilling God's plan—to reach physical humankind. You and I are the church. It is our responsibility to carry out the plan of reaching people with the gospel. That is the Matthew 6:33 principle.

I want to amplify this notion to drive home the truth that God needs us. Because His kingdom—where He dwells—is spiritual, His laws are spiritual. In fact, everything about God is spiritual (John 4:24: "God is spirit, and his worshipers must worship in spirit and in truth"). The following thoughts are intended to challenge our thinking that God needs us.

How would you describe God's kingdom, His abode, without using church lingo? That's simply a rhetorical question for the purpose of challenging your mind. Let's refer to a place where God dwells as "heaven" for the sake of our study: it's a place of organization, protocols, an echelon of leadership, a place where the will of God is absolute law and is carried out explicitly, a place where His motives are not questioned, His Word is law, and He is trusted implicitly. It is a place of beauty, peace, and joy unspeakable. The whole scenario is spiritual in nature, whereas our existence is material. Each works under different laws.

When we speak of kingdom rule, we refer to the beautiful rule of the Holy Spirit. I believe that was God's rule in the Garden of Eden, until Satan injected his suggestions into Eve and convinced her and Adam that God was not completely trustworthy. Satan convinced Adam and Eve that there was a better way to attain a good life than the way God had laid out for them. From that time forward, kingdom rule did not exist on earth.

With this mind-set the stage is prepared for understanding the concept of this book. It is God's plan to bring His chosen people under kingdom rule. He chose the small nation of Israel to display God's sovereignty, His rule: to prove to the world that He exists and wants to be eminent on earth. That is really what the Old Testament is about. Israel kept failing God in His purpose, however.

It is important to keep in mind the basic difference between heaven's laws and earth's laws. Humankind depends mostly on what is seen, heard, or felt. Because God's realm is spiritual, it is not easy for God to communicate with us, so He chose a human channel through whom He could work: a channel that would be obedient to Him, someone in whom He could inject His nature, His power, His will. Israel was that choice, but Israel wanted to be like other nations, free from depending on a supernatural being. It's typical of human nature to desire the freedom to control life.

The Old Testament gives a clear picture of God proving to Israel His desire to care for them, to direct, protect, and supply all their needs. He chose individual men and women—prophets, judges, and other leaders—to channel His message and keep Israel on track, but to no avail. They kept failing God in their mission, and therefore God set Israel aside for a while and grafted in another element to fulfill His mission: the church of the Lord Jesus Christ—called *ecclesia*—"the called-out body" (Romans 11:13–25).

It could be construed that God was disappointed in Israel and made a mistake in trusting His mission to Israel, that their failure was an "oops" to God, that it slipped up on Him and He revised His plan with the church.

Nothing could be further from the truth. Everything that was written aforetime was written for our learning of the scripture for our comfort and hope (Romans 15:4). It was all in the plan of God. Nothing slips up on God; He is alpha and omega, the beginning and the end. If it had not been for God bringing about the church of Jesus Christ, you and I would have been left out of the picture. God has the whole picture in view. At a later date (after the tribulation period), God will pick Israel up and put her back on track.

Each believer should love God and desire to see Him pleased. Reading accounts of Israel and Judah in the Old Testament makes us wonder how they could have mistreated God as they did. God wanted to bless Israel and Judah. He did, in many ways and at many times. He wanted the world to know that there is a living God. Yet, Israel and Judah kept failing to help God accomplish His goal.

Does it create a desire in your heart, as it does in mine, to help God accomplish His purpose on earth? If that is our desire, then it pleases Him to help us in our efforts. God is perpetually looking for men and women who will stand with Him in His purpose. We are human and will make mistakes and veer off course at times, but He knows the bent of our heart. The view I have been presenting is the foundation of the Matthew 6:33 principle.

When believers stumble the Holy Spirit will gently guide them back on course, dust them off, give them a gentle pat, and encourage another try. He knows our infirmities and will help fulfill a desire to work with our loving Father. The Holy Spirit knows the mind of the Father (Romans 8:26–27).

The church is God's emissary on earth for the purpose of being a witness to Jesus Christ (Acts 1:8). The church consists of born-again believers, filled with the Holy Spirit. God's plan for the church is to fulfill what He wanted Israel to accomplish: to prove to the world that God exists and desires to be involved with His creation (Hebrews 11:6).

After the church has completed the task God has set for it, God will remove it from the earth and place Israel back into operation. The church is the main thrust at the moment. Therefore, we will dedicate the next chapter to the subject of church. Remember, you and I are the church, the kingdom of God on earth.

(CHAPTER TEN)

The Church

Ecclesia—the called-out body (the church of the Lord Jesus Christ)—was born on the day of Pentecost (a Jewish agricultural festival that traditionally took place fifty days after the beginning of Passover), when the Holy Spirit came and took up residence in believers. This event occurred fifty days after Jesus' death and resurrection (Acts 2:1: "When the day of Pentecost came, they were all together in one place").

This concept might challenge your theology, but give it some thought. When Jesus Christ won the battle over Satan in the Garden of Gethsemane, the Cross and Resurrection, He defeated Satan in an arena of humanity, thus giving God freedom or a legal right to send the Holy Spirit to earth to reside in believers "Up to that time the Holy Spirit had not been given, since Jesus had not yet been glorified" (John 7:39).

Jesus showed himself to His apostles forty days after His resurrection, telling them not to leave Jerusalem until the Holy Spirit came and baptized them (Acts 1:2–5). On the day of Pentecost a phenomenon happened: the Holy Spirit came to earth and settled on all the believers that were assembled together (Acts 2:1–4). This was a significant day. It was the day the church was born—it was a new day in God's plan for earth.

(It's interesting to note that organizations that are predicated upon a doctrinal belief in baptism in the Holy Spirit, as a second work of grace, call themselves "Pentecostal," deriving their name from the experience described in Acts 2:4.)

Now, back to God's purpose for the church: it is the same purpose God had for Israel. To be a witness, proving to humanity that God exists. God wants to bring kingdom rule to earth. God has now changed His method from Israel to the ecclesia, the church. The church begins with the New Covenant (New Testament). The New Covenant consisted of God being with us as Immanuel (Matthew 1:23). "God the Son" was born into the flow of human history. After His death and resurrection, then "God the Holy Spirit" came to fill believers' lives so as to be witnesses to Jesus Christ (Acts 1:8).

There was a significant change in God's method on earth. Christ was sent in the person of Jesus to build a spiritual kingdom, rather than an earthly kingdom, in the form of a "true church" made up of Holy Spirit–filled individuals.

I reiterate that the kingdom of heaven is an earthly, physical aspect of the kingdom of God—buildings, denominations, organizations, stained glass windows, altars, and so forth. The physical components make up a husk around the fruit. The genuine kingdom of God is in the heart of a believer. One day the husk, the organized church, and the true church, the fruit, shall be separated (Mark 4:26–29).

At this time, the true body of Christ shall go to meet the Lord in the air (1 Thessalonians 4:13–17). The organized church shall continue here on earth—it will be an anti-Christ, world church, a church in which Jesus and all other world-accepted prophets and leaders are recognized, but Jesus will not be recognized as the Christ. The world church shall be in accord with the world government, described in scripture as the beast (political) and the false prophet as the church (Revelation 19:20: "But the beast was captured and with him the false prophet who had performed the miraculous signs on his behalf").

Keep in mind that this is my interpretation concerning the church and the end time (eschatology). It is my conviction that without Jesus being the Christ, there is no redemption. It requires the Holy Spirit in an individual to recognize Jesus as the Christ (Romans 8:9; Matthew 16:13–18; John 3:3–8). When the Holy Spirit is removed from earth, the organized church will not recognize Jesus as the Christ. Therefore, the church will be a false prophet.

The kingdom of God on earth (the church) is sometimes called an interlude of grace between the time when God calls a halt to Israel as His witness and when He picks Israel up again after the tribulation period. It must be remembered that God does not discard Israel. He only sets her aside for a while (Romans 6). The church is God's witness for now. Jesus Christ is head of the church, and the Holy Spirit is the power in believers' lives.

We have established thus far that Spirit-filled persons are the church of Jesus Christ. The church is designed to be a witness to God's reality and power. He is worthy of trust, praise, and honor. The Holy Spirit is encouraging an expansion of the kingdom of God—into the hearts of new believers. The mandate from Jesus Christ was to evangelize the world; it was the last message that He left to the church (Matthew 28:18–20).

I want to emphasize three points about the church of Jesus Christ:

- It is our responsibility and privilege to be witnesses;
- We are to evangelize and make converts to Jesus Christ (Matthew 28:19–20);
- We are to mature into Christlike people so that the world can see Christ-centered lives—again, we are to serve as witnesses (Ephesians 4:11–13).

Thus far I have not said anything about those people who refuse to accept Jesus Christ as their savior. What shall be their fate? The picture is so dismal that it is beyond the power of words to describe. Hell is a place of torment. Time there is without end. For any human being to wind up in such a place would be the tragedy of all tragedies.

When all that is required to avoid hell is to accept Jesus Christ as God's slain lamb who paid the supreme sacrifice for our sins, there really is no excuse for anyone going to hell (Romans 10:8–13). If you are reading this book and have not made peace with God through Jesus Christ, now would be an excellent time to do so.

The dispensation of grace—church age—is a display of God's mercy. His mercy and grace were inserted into the flow of human history in the person of Jesus Christ for a designated period of time. Any person who has faith in Jesus Christ and His sacrifice will enjoy a special place in eternity (1 Peter 2:9; the Bride of Christ, Revelation 21:9–27). Allow your mind, for a moment, to meditate on the privilege of being part of the glorious church, the bride of Christ, the New Jerusalem. What an awful mistake it would be to miss such an opportunity.

Reflect on the following questions:

- How long before God's clock starts running again for Israel?
- What will happen to the church? It has been more than two thousand years since the dispensation of grace, the church age, began.
- What happens to Spirit-filled folks who have died?

These are valid questions that the Bible answers for us. I shall give a synopsis of the plan, but it would be well for you to delve into God's Word for an in-depth study on your own.

Now consider the following responses:

- The invitation is open for each individual until death; after that, eternity is settled. It is appointed unto us once to die, but after this comes the judgment (Hebrews 9:27: "Just

as man is destined to die once and after that to face judgment"). Sounds final, does it not?
- How long is the dispensation of grace—the church age—open? It's open until Jesus returns in the clouds, to receive the church, including those that have died in Christ and those remaining alive at the time of His return (1 Corinthians 15:51–57; 1 Thessalonians 4:13–18). This event is referred to as the "rapture" of the church.
- Those who have died in Christ shall receive a resurrected body, analogous to Jesus Christ's resurrected body.
- In the twinkling of an eye, Christians living at that time shall have their bodies changed into resurrected bodies.
- All shall rise to meet Jesus Christ in the air and return with Him, to whatever He has planned (1 Thessalonians 4:17: "After that, we who are still alive and are left will be caught up together with them in the clouds to meet the Lord in the air. And so we will be with the Lord forever").

Whatever you do in life, don't miss the rapture. That's my word on the matter.

What about the resumption of God's time clock for Israel? The next events are subjects of serious debate among theologians and Bible scholars. I shall give my interpretation of coming events that are acceptable in most evangelical churches. You must be your own judge.

We have projected to you in the previous paragraphs about the coming of the Lord Jesus Christ for His church. Now I am presenting to you a different event.

The "Day of the Lord" (2 Thessalonians 2:1–12) will not be short lived. It will begin when the church is removed from earth and will continue until the end of the present earth's existence, the length of time to be one thousand years.

After the church is removed, which is the restraining force against evil, then the man of sin, the Antichrist, is revealed and trouble begins on earth like nothing ever experienced before. It is called Jacob's

Trouble (read Jeremiah 30:1–7). You will see why the United States has stood with Israel all these years and why most of the Middle East hates the United States—because of our loyalty to Israel.

Somewhere near the end of the seven years, Jesus Christ returns with the resurrected saints and destroys the enemies of God. He sets up His earthly kingdom and reigns for a millennium. Satan will be bound for that period of time. All this is designed to bring Israel back into God's favor and Jesus Christ as the Messiah. God does not give up on people, does He?

Before leaving this discussion of the "church," I direct your attention to an interesting study found in Revelation 1:19–3:22. Jesus Christ is talking with John while John is under the influence of the Holy Spirit (Revelation 2:10–11). The message is to be written to the seven existing churches on earth. We are given an insight concerning the time frame of the message (Revelation 1:19): "Write the things which thou hast seen, and the things which are, and the things which shall be hereafter." Immediately, Jesus delves into the messages to the churches, and they continue to Revelation 3:22. I submit that the time frame covers the conditions of churches during John's lifetime and during and following the present church age.

By carefully studying each of the seven churches, we can detect conditions that have plagued the church community. We are able to determine how Christ feels about each condition (Revelation 4:1). Note how the scene shifts from earth to heaven and the invitation for John to come up there, to learn what happens next. We do not see the church mentioned again—it has been removed from earth.

This is my interpretation of these scenes. You must make your own determination on all these scriptures. I realize how far-out all this seems. It all defies good reasoning, but we must remember that everything about God is supernatural. The Bible is the supernaturally inspired Word of God. It is received only by faith.

We shall title the next chapter "Faith," a small word but one that means so much more than at first meets the eye.

(CHAPTER ELEVEN)

Faith

Faith is the central theme of the Bible. I best describe my view of faith by comparing it to eyesight. Eyesight is a capacity and when it is lost, a valuable quality is gone. Eyesight observes physical objects. Faith is also a way of seeing, but one designed to observe spiritual subjects; without faith it is impossible to please God (Hebrews 11:6). Faith is the eye of the inner person.

Faith is a gift from God that allows us to observe intangible objects; it is capable of translating the intangible into the tangible. In the natural world, when someone gives you a pencil it is evident that you have the pencil: you can see and feel the pencil.

Faith allows us to have and see the pencil before it is physically evident (Hebrews 11:1: "Now faith is the substance of things hoped for, the evidence of things not seen"; King James Version). I refer to faith as God's gift of sight so that we can see spiritual subjects—it is heavenly eyesight.

Without faith sight, everything about God is dark, completely hidden from us. Without faith:

- The Bible is nothing more than stories of history and fables.
- The resurrection of Jesus Christ is only a myth.

- Salvation through the blood of Jesus Christ is a scheme thought up by human beings.
- Life after death is a fancy story only children should believe.
- A living God who made everything and rules Heaven and earth is beyond belief.

It requires God-given faith to see the reality of these things (Hebrews 11:6). In fact, Hebrews 11 gives us a vivid description of how powerful faith sight really is.

Redemption through Jesus Christ is the most important subject known to an individual, being justified in the sight of Almighty God. Being exonerated of all our sins is more than we can understand. Yet we receive that exoneration with joy unspeakable because of God's gift of faith (Ephesians 2:8–9).

Faith is a target of our enemy, Satan. If he can destroy our faith, he can separate us from Jesus Christ and our hope of eternal life. It is essential to realize that faith is a gift from God (Ephesians 2:8); we must protect it and work at increasing our level of faith.

"God hath dealt to every man the measure of faith" (Romans 12:3 King James Version). It appears that the measure is only a starter and that each individual must decide what he or she is going to do with the starter gift of faith. A starter is capable of increasing, but it must come in contact with a common denominator, analogous to a snowball rolling in snow. The only common denominator to God's gift of faith is the Word of God (Romans 10:17: "So then faith comes by hearing, and hearing by the word of God"; King James Version). We must be diligent in adding to our faith; growing in faith assures us of never faltering in our relationship with God (2 Peter 1:2–10).

Jesus warned us that Satan's primary goal is to kill, steal, and destroy (John 10:10). What is his target? It's our faith. He cannot destroy us unless we give in to his suggestions. Maintaining a strong faith defeats the enemy (Ephesians 6:11–17). Therefore, Satan's primary target is our faith. If he can destroy our faith, kill our faith, rob us of our faith, he has accomplished his mission. We are encouraged to "put on the full armor of God" so that "you can take your stand against the devil's schemes" (Ephesians 6:11).

The one piece of armor that is most prominent in this passage is the shield of faith: "above all, taking the shield of faith with which you shall be able to quench all the fiery darts of the wicked one" (Ephesians 6:16 King James Version).

More than fifty years of ministry has led me to believe that faith is one of the most misunderstood subjects in the Word of God. Why is it misunderstood? Because faith is so vital to a child of God, and the enemy works overtime to harm it and cause confusion on the subject.

Some common errors in misunderstanding faith:

- Making faith its own object—having faith in faith.
- Feeling that if we can "get" enough faith we can receive our healing.
- Feeling that if we can get enough faith we can move the hand of God.
- Believing that a loved one died because one did not have enough faith.

Having this conception of faith generally leads to disappointment. Situations arise when God will not answer our requests, not because our faith level is low, but because it is not His will to grant our request at that moment (1 John 5:14–15). The enemy will accuse us of not having enough faith and will try to convince us that God is not pleased with us. Satan is a liar: God loves us and has a better plan for us. Our faith must be in God—not in our faith.

A common mistake regarding faith comes from measuring our faith level by whether or not God answers our requests. Our faith in God should stay firm when our requests are not answered in a way we expect or desire (Habakkuk 3:17–19).

The more we fill our mind and soul with truth about God, the stronger our faith becomes. That's the reason for absorbing the Word of God and having a prayer life.

If I left us at this point on faith there would be times when we would be further confused. There will be times when we observe someone praying a prayer of faith that moves the hand of God ("The prayer of faith shall save the sick"; James 5:13–18 King James Version). To keep a clear picture on this subject we must remember that faith is a gift from God. We can increase our faith through prescribed methods, but we must not try to override God's will with our faith. Whenever God wants something accomplished, He will give faith to someone to fulfill His will (1 Corinthians 12:4–11). God's gifts are to profit His will (1 John 5:14–15). The secret is to find the will of God on any matter.

Anything short of the sovereignty of God requires faith on our part. What do I mean by the sovereignty of God? Sovereignty refers to the supremacy of God's will. When God wills something to happen, He causes it to occur, without faith on any person's part, for example:

- When God spoke the world into existence;
- When God created humankind;
- When Jesus Christ came into the world;
- When Jesus Christ died on the cross; and
- When Jesus Christ rose from the grave (the Resurrection).

All these events occurred without faith on any human being's part. In fact, humankind did not grasp their significance when they did occur.

God created the faith system to separate people who want God in their lives from those who do not. Faith might be compared to a ticket, as an means of admittance. Without (the ticket of) faith, it is impossible to please God (Hebrews 11:6). God rewards living faith. (I trust you realize I am paraphrasing this particular scripture.)

Faith must be tested to determine its validity and to ascertain its strength (1 Peter 1:3–9). I draw your attention to Jesus' words to Peter, recorded in Luke 22:31–32: "Simon, Simon, behold, Satan hath desired to have you, that he may sift you as wheat. But I have prayed for you that your faith fail not. And when you are converted, strengthen your brethren." Jesus prayed that Peter's faith would stand the test.

Faith is so vital to us that it behooves each of us to protect our faith, with all the tools God has given us (1 Peter 1:3–10; Ephesians 6:11–18). Faith in Jesus Christ is our ticket to eternal life. Make sure yours is valid.

Jesus had an interesting and enlightening conversation with some folks who witnessed His feeding five thousand people on five barley loaves and two small fishes. The people followed Jesus with a definite plan. They wanted to do what He had just done. They thought it would be great if they could produce that kind of miracle. Jesus told them that they were not interested in the miracle, they simply wanted the food. He was pointing them to eternal life, instead of seeking material things.

Jesus reinforced the message concerning faith: "This is the work of God: that you believe on Him whom God sent" (John 6:26–29). It all seems so simple. We humans, on the other hand, have the conception that if it doesn't cost a lot it can't be very valuable. We are convinced that it must be much more complicated than that.

The truth of the matter is that it does cost more than meets the eye. Accepting Jesus Christ as redeemer requires that we change our lifestyle and follow the teachings of God's Word. However, the change is gradual under the leadership of the Holy Spirit. Many people make the mistake of thinking they must clean up their lives before coming to Christ. When we have faith in Christ as God's Son, the rest will come.

(CHAPTER TWELVE)

The Two Minds

> That He would grant you, according to the riches of His glory, to be strengthened with might by His Spirit in the inner man. (EPHESIANS 3:16)

In this chapter we are focusing on two minds in each person: the biological, physical brain and the inner mind, the spiritual, subliminal, subconscious mind. I am not a psychologist, so I will treat this subject from a biblical viewpoint.

We aren't referring to Christians exclusively, but to all of humankind. There's a spiritual side as well as a physical side to every human being. The medical community, psychiatry, deals in the subconscious mind, beyond the physical mind or brain. Psychiatry and psychology have made a great deal of progress in understanding this discipline over the past fifty years, but humanity is limited in fully understanding the soul and its attributes. We are limited in our understanding of a spiritual mind, but the Bible keeps reminding us of the spiritual side of life.

Numerous times Jesus makes the statement that "if any man has ears to hear, let him hear" (Mark 4:23). I don't believe He is referring to physical hearing. He is addressing inner hearing belonging to the inner person. Paul in his writings addresses the inner man quite often. In 2 Corinthians 4:16-18, for example, he tells us that the outward man is perishing, "For which cause we faint not; but though our outward man perish, yet the inward man is renewed day by day" (King James Version). He is telling us to keep in view the life in the Spirit, seen not with the natural eye but with the eyes of the eternal.

Our spiritual mind belongs to the soul. Our soul contains emotions, desires, and will, elements that regulate much of our physical activity. Jesus Christ came into this world to seek and save our souls—the inner mind of the inner person. Our physical body and brain shall not inherit the kingdom of God; it shall return to the soil from which it came. When Jesus Christ returns for His Church at the time of the rapture, all Christians alive at the time shall be changed in an instant to resurrected bodies (1 Corinthians 15:50–53). Our physical bodies and mental capacity could not handle supernatural life.

The Holy Spirit dwells in the inner person of a born-again child of God. It is our inner mind the Holy Spirit is working to change. Our inner mind must be trained, as well as our physical mind. Before a person is born again by the Spirit of God, the inner mind is an enemy to God and His Spiritual laws, dwelling and meditating on destructive thoughts. Our physical mind picks up inspirations and suggestions from our inner mind; our body carries out the activities (Romans 8:5–11).

Until a person has a spiritual birth in his or her inner mind, that person cannot see or understand spiritual matters (John 3:3–21). Nicodemus was a very religious person, but he didn't have a spiritual birth in his inner mind. Jesus is pointing out to Nicodemus that a physical mind can have religious training, as Nicodemus did, but it will not understand spiritual things—the things that are of God.

There are many people today in the same condition as Nicodemus. They are extremely religious, follow all their churches' doctrines, but had never had a spiritual awakening in their inner being. They attend church and try to worship God, but it is empty worship—there's something missing. Religious-minded (not born-again) people try to worship God by physical activities. They go through the motions physically, but it falls short of true worship, unless the Holy Spirit activates their inner beings to worship.

The inner mind—the inner person with the Holy Spirit—is able to truly worship God (John 4:23–24: "'Yet a time is coming and has now come when the true worshipers will worship the Father in spirit and truth, for they are the kind of worshipers the Father seeks. God is spirit, and his worshipers must worship in spirit and in truth'"). It is important to explain something at this point: many times when true worship is in operation, human beings will go through similar physical activities that people do when it is not true worship, such as raising their hands, clapping their hands, and other sorts of worshipful motions. They all may be involved in what their church teaches about physical activity during worship time. It is difficult to determine who is involved in true worship and who is not. We must refrain from judging other people in their worship. God alone knows the heart of each individual.

Anyone reading what I have just said in the preceding two paragraphs could easily misconstrue the concept of true worship versus physical worship. We must always remember that we are physical beings, even though "born-again." We still exercise our free will. The Holy Spirit will never override our will by force. He will never force us to worship God against our will. The Holy Spirit may speak to us in that still inner voice, or He may inspire us, but He will not force us.

How can I know whether to engage in some activity, such as raising my hands during church worship services? Should I wait until the Holy Spirit moves me to the activity? My answer to this question is the main reason for this paragraph. As human beings, we worship God out of our will rather than emotion. If God's Word tells us that it is proper to exercise activity, then we are right to enter into the activity, even though we don't feel inspired to do so. We activate our action out of honor and praise to our God by obedience. True worship is not in the activity but in our obedience.

It is appropriate to consider those in authority during a church service. We may be accustomed to a particular activity in our regular worship services, but now we find ourselves in a church gathering where those activities are inappropriate. Should I go ahead and activate my physical worship? No. We must worship God by our obedience to those who have authority over us at the moment (Romans 12 and 13; 1 Corinthians 8:1–13). These passages should be understood as principles, rather than focusing on a particular mentioned problem. For instance, Paul is talking about food being offensive to a brother or sister. It would be the same regarding anything that offends our brother or sister in Christ.

If you find yourself in a group that does not agree with your doctrine, don't make a fuss about the difference; simply stay away next time. Don't make a scene. They may be more correct than you.

The inner person, the inner mind, is where the Holy Spirit dwells and works to bring us into a way of living that God intends for us. The Bible uses two words to help us understand God's action in our lives through which He brings us into a relationship with Him.

The first word is *justification*: when we receive Jesus Christ as our redeemer, by faith, then we have right standing with God our Father, as if we had never sinned. We are justified before God (Romans 5:1–2: "Therefore, since we have been justified through faith, we have peace with God through our Lord Jesus Christ").

The second word is *sanctification*, which comes from the same Greek word meaning *holy*, "to be set apart for a particular use." A process of sanctification begins when we are born into the kingdom of God through Christ Jesus, and it continues throughout our lifetime. Little by little our inner person is being tutored by the Holy Spirit to bring us into an image of Jesus Christ. The change that occurs is gradual and proceeds as we are obedient to the Holy Spirit's direction and God's Word (Romans 6:1–23).

Sanctification begins in the inner person and works its way outward in the form of physical action and character. Paul gives us an insight into Christ dwelling within us through the Holy Spirit. Paul is saying that he (Paul) is physically alive, but the life Paul is living is produced by Christ within Paul (Galatians 2:20: "I have been crucified with Christ and no longer live, but Christ lives in me. The life I live in the body, I live by faith in the Son of God, who loved me and gave himself for me"). We should realize that Christian character is not mere moral correctness, but the possession and manifestation of graces working within us through the Holy Spirit in our inner person (Galatians 5:22–26: "But the fruit of the Spirit is love, joy, peace, longsuffering, gentleness, goodness, faith, meekness, self control; against such there is no law. And they that are Christ's have crucified the flesh with the affections and lusts. If we live in the Spirit, let us also walk in the Spirit. Let us not be desirous of vainglory, provoking one another, envying one another"; King James Version).

When we receive Jesus Christ as our redeemer, something occurs within us: the Holy Spirit takes up residency within us. The Holy Spirit begins a sanctification process to change our old nature into a new one that God has planned for us (2 Corinthians 5:17–6:1). We are now destined to be workers with Christ Jesus as His ambassadors.

"We are now Jesus Christ's workmanship, through the Holy Spirit, created in Christ Jesus unto good works, which God has before ordained that we should walk in them" (Ephesians 2:10). We no longer belong to ourselves; we belong to Jesus Christ, who purchased us at a great price (1 Corinthians 6:19–20).

Many Christian people go through life believing they can live as they please, not really giving much thought to being workers with Jesus Christ to carry out His plan on earth, never considering that they are to be instruments of righteousness (Romans 6:8–23). Because they are not seeking first the kingdom of God and His righteousness, their life is void of the promises that God has given to us in His Word (Matthew 6:33).

I am convinced that all born-again persons, struggling and not living abundant lives, could change their situation by making a decision to obey the Holy Spirit and God's Word concerning God's plan for us (Psalm 1:1–3).

We should give thought to what Jesus Christ's desires are. Each of us should ask him- or herself: What does He want to accomplish through me? Am I helping Jesus perform the responsibility that God our Father trusted Him to do? Although my capabilities may be meager, I give them to Jesus Christ for His use (2 Timothy 2:19–21).

If we have this kind of mind-set, we shall have a faith in God that will bring answers to our needs. Why? Because our concerns are God's interests and not for our own self-serving desires.

God does not judge the quantity of our talents. He judges according to our obedience in using the talents we possess. Comparison is a human function that is obnoxious to God. In God's divine wisdom He creates each of us with certain gifts, and He expects us to use those gifts for His benefit. If we all had the same gifts, the kingdom of God would suffer. It takes all the gifts to complete God's picture.

Paul uses our physical body to illustrate this crucial point. The body of Christ is one, but it has many members. "If the foot shall say, 'because I am not the hand I am not of the body,' is it therefore not of the body?" Paul continues in this vein, using the various body parts to elucidate the significance of understanding all God's gifts to build His kingdom. Every member in the body is vital to its wellbeing. When one lags, hurts, or disrupts, the entire body suffers (1 Corinthians 12:12–27).

Let us carry this concept a step further for the purpose of showing the essence of avoiding disruption in the body of Christ. Many times in churches disruption is instigated by a member who is unhappy about something. The unrest builds until the whole body is ill. When one member isn't functioning properly, it affects the entire body. In our natural body the member of the body that is malfunctioning must be treated, if possible, and removed if treatment fails. Jesus Christ gives us instructions for handling this sort of problem in the church (Matthew 18:15–17). Many times problems arise within church bodies because someone's feelings are hurt. Many times a person wants to be recognized as the equal of someone else in the body—maybe the person is a little jealous of someone else's ministry or of the appreciation given to another.

Wouldn't life be great if we truly understood that we don't have to measure up to others—Billy Graham, Charles Stanley, Oral Roberts, our pastor, or teacher, or anybody? They have their ministry, and we have ours.

It is of paramount importance for each of us to understand that we are unique. Our usefulness in life depends upon being what we are designed to be. The weight of trying to live up to someone else's standard is the cause of many failures. Jesus Christ came to reach each and every one of us with His plan of redemption. He will put each of us in touch with who God designed us to be. We are individuals. You will never be so free in life as you are when you simply be yourself, in Christ (John 8:36: "'So if the Son sets you free, you will be free indeed'").

(CHAPTER THIRTEEN)

What Is My Gift?

Over fifty-nine years of teaching seminars and filling pastoral positions, I think the question people ask more than any other is, "What is my ministry—what is my gift?" They truly want to work with Jesus Christ, but don't believe they are gifted or qualified for ministry. They live defeated lives believing they are second-class citizens in God's vineyard.

We devote this chapter to those who struggle with this question. I prayerfully trust that these thoughts and biblical references will revolutionize your life. God loves you; He ordained that you would have work in His vineyard (Ephesians 2:10).

The enemy has done a superb job of confusing the ministry of Jesus Christ by defining the ministry as preachers, teachers, pastors, evangelists, and so forth. There are as many different ministries as there are Christians. The Bible enumerates several, but the list is by no means exhaustive. Paul tells us to present our bodies a living sacrifice, holy, acceptable unto God, which is our reasonable service. And to not conform to this world, but be transformed by the renewing of our minds that we may "prove what is that good and acceptable and perfect will of God" (Romans 12:1–2).

We must not allow human thinking to convince us that we do not have a ministry. God has given every born-again person a gift to be used in the work of God—we must have faith to believe that. "For by the grace given me I say to every one of you: Do not think of yourself more highly than you ought, but rather think of yourself with sober judgment, in accordance with the measure of faith God has given you" (Romans 12:3). I encourage you to think about your past and consider the times when you have had an effect on people, maybe a word of encouragement, a prayer life that changes situations, a heart of compassion that reaches out to hurting folks, a cup of cold water to someone thirsty (an illustration of doing something nice and uplifting), maybe only a smile. These are only a few illustrations to challenge your thinking. We all have something about us that can be uplifting to others.

Romans 12:4–21 suggests many different ideas of ministry. We can deduce from this passage that ministries are limitless. As we meditate on this subject, the Holy Spirit will remind us of times when we have helped someone. We begin realizing that there have been many such times, until we start forming an idea about where God wants to use us. We will look for opportunities to use our gift that God has endowed us with, a gift that we did not realize was valuable.

Maybe you will be sitting in church listening to an evangelist, your pastor, or teacher, and the Holy Spirit will give to you a thought, challenging you to some seemingly insignificant ministry. Do not ignore the thought or allow it to pass without doing something about the Holy Spirit's inspiration. As you mull over a thought, later it shall become greater. An opportunity will present itself to be used in the ministry of the kingdom of God. By faith we make our lives available to God for His use (Ephesians 4:11–16).

The most effective ministries happen in everyday situations, at home, on the job, in the marketplace, over a cup of coffee, in friendly visits or social gatherings, through a letter or a phone call. They are not in a church setting at all. We are the church wherever we are; we have the Holy Spirit with us every hour of every day. The Holy Spirit is always about the Father's business, and we are coworkers with Him.

You are God's property in Christ Jesus. Therefore, you are special and have an extraordinary gift designed for you. Even your fingerprints are distinctive. Everything about you is uncommon. You may have believed that you were not valuable because you have compared yourself to others. You may be comparing your gift to other folks' gifts. When we compare our gifts to those of others, we always come up short because their gifts are unique to them. You are a minister ordained by God Himself. Now, allow Him to lead you into using that gift to further His kingdom.

The title of this book, *The Matthew 6:33 Principle*, and the subsequent exposition are heavily slanted toward having a good life here and now, which Jesus Christ did teach. I would be remiss, however, if I left out the most significant teaching of our Lord and the basic reason for His coming. He came to seek and to save lost souls. The Father is not willing that any human being should perish or be lost from His presence (2 Peter 3:9). This subject is much more important than having a good life on earth.

Generally speaking, many human beings make a decision to come to Christ motivated by some physical need. My decision was prompted by my utter failure to take care of my family. Others may come as the result of an illness, fear of the future, or a relationship gone sour. The reasons that God uses to attract human attention can be endless.

When reading the life of Christ, it is interesting to note how many times He met some physical need first, before dealing with the spiritual problem. Observing that principle, it's easy to understand why Jesus used the Matthew 6:33 principle to attract so many people. It's virtually impossible to study the "Matthew 6:33" concept without it leading to a hunger or desire for eternal life.

(CHAPTER FOURTEEN)

The Law of Life

(Deuteronomy 28:1–68)

The word *Deuteronomy* literally means "the law restated." The Hebrew title is "Debarim," meaning "The Book of the Words." When we reduce this to our way of understanding, it means that God's words are restated concerning His laws of life. God laid down laws pertaining to life, and if we understand and obey those laws, an abundant life is promised. The first fourteen verses of Deuteronomy 28 are positive regarding an abundant life—if human beings obey the laws. The next fifty-four verses describe the miserable and negative life that will result from breaking those laws.

Humanity decided to circumvent God's laws right from the start (Genesis 3). The devil became prince of this world (in John 14:30, Jesus says, "I will not speak with you much longer, for the prince of this world is coming. He has no hold on me"). From that time human beings tried to have an abundant life, separate from God's laws. For a while humans think they are succeeding and then something happens, causing failure.

An interesting story of a man thinking he can run his own life goes like this: He said to God, "I am a farmer and I could do a better job than you do, if you'd let me control the weather."

God said, "Let's try it."

The farmer prepared his field for planting corn. He told God, "Don't send any rain until I get the seed in the ground."

The seed was put into the ground, and then the farmer asked God to send rain.

"I don't want a gully washer, just a *zoon, zoon* drizzle."

God sent a gentle rain.

The corn grew big and beautiful. The field was the best the farmer had ever seen. He said to God, "Don't send any rain until I cultivate the field and lay it by, so the corn can grow without weeds."

God held up the rain, and everything was on schedule—just great.

The field was ready for harvest. It was a beauty to behold. Looked like a bumper crop.

When the time came to harvest, it turned out there wasn't one ear of corn on the stalks.

The farmer asked God, "What's wrong with my crop of corn?"

God said, "You forgot to ask for pollination when the corn was teaseling."

We are not equipped to succeed without God's hand (Malachi 3:7–14). God promised to favor us with His blessings, providing we obey God's laws. God's laws are established, and we cannot change them or circumvent them, regardless of the amount of technology we accumulate. We must learn to work with God's laws. For instance, gravity is one of God's laws. If we attempt to defy or ignore gravity, we will be destroyed.

Jesus said, "I came to undo the works of the devil, so you can have an abundant life" (John 10:10). The enemy wants to encourage us to believe that obeying God is a religion and that it has little bearing on real life, here and now. The devil would have us believe that if we do accept Christ and obey God's Word, our reward is after death and is not valuable for this life. He figures that somewhere between accepting Christ and when we die, he can discourage us and we will give up (he certainly does try that).

Matthew 6:33 is God's promise that if we will seek His kingdom and obey His laws, an abundant life will flow to us. Why are there so many Christians who follow Christ and are called by His name and yet are not blessed? It could be because they have made God's gift of eternal life into a religious endeavor instead of a way of life.

An interesting point is found in Philippians 4:5: "Let your gentleness be evident to all." Moderation encompasses the lack of excess—being well balanced in our lifestyle. The Lord is at hand. Having balance brings God into every part of our life. Reading the rest of Philippians 4 guides us into proper thinking and action—then the God of peace will be with us.

Human nature has a propensity toward becoming unbalanced. Most of us are inclined toward overindulgence in some area of life, perhaps even regarding things that are considered to be good. Can we become unbalanced in pursuing some religious activity? Of course we can, unless we define religious activity as practical help and kindness toward our fellow human beings.

There is, for example, a danger in giving to others, in the name of religion, and yet letting our own family suffer from lack (Matthew 15:5–6: "'But you say that if a man says to his father or mother, "Whatever help you might otherwise have received from me is a gift devoted to God," he is not to "honor his father" with it. Thus you nullify the word of God for the sake of your tradition'"). Or, we may give to the church but fail to pay our bills. Both come under the heading of religion that is unbalanced.

Humankind's interpretation pertaining to religion can take many avenues. That is why there are many different religions. It's intrinsic for humanity's pendulum to swing too far one way or the other. For instance, God's Word is explicit about helping those in need. It is part of God's plan for His followers, yet some religions make this their way of salvation, leaving out a born-again experience by faith in Jesus Christ. Both are important functions and should be exercised in balance. The physical function is an outgrowth of the inward experience.

In Romans 14:17–23, Paul is addressing a religious problem

that is out of balance. Rather than laws controlling food and drink being a sign of religion, Paul is teaching that there are more important considerations to the kingdom of God. "The kingdom of God is not food and drink, but righteousness and peace and joy in the Holy Spirit."

Righteousness is having Jesus Christ in the heart, through the born-again experience, and then the peace of God that comes from having right standing with God. The joy of the Lord is our strength (Nehemiah 8:10) in the Holy Spirit. If you will observe, not one of these concepts—peace, right standing, joy—is physical; they are spiritually based. Yet we see in reading the rest of the chapter (19–23) that Paul is teaching that our actions can be wrong if what we do offends another person. Perhaps you are alone and eat or drink something and it does not affect your faith negatively. But if you were with someone who might be vexed by your action, then it would be wrong to do it. That would not be considered hypocritical but considerate.

Our focus in this chapter is on "the laws of life." There are physical laws and there are spiritual laws. If we break physical laws (for example, by consistently eating poorly), we suffer the physical consequences (bad health). We may get away with it for a while, but eventually we pay the price. If we behave badly toward others, we will have broken relationships. If we don't pay our bills, we develop a faulty credit rating. Buying things impulsively will eventually destroy our chances of financial success.

Breaking physical laws will result in a negative lifestyle. Many people think they can routinely violate physical laws and still have a good life. A person would have a better chance of winning the lottery than enjoying a good life if they break these laws. We reap what we sow.

There are spiritual laws that must be obeyed. When these are violated, consequences occur. Second Peter 1:3–10 clearly states how these laws work. If we are prudent in following the prescribed method, we can expect a successful and peaceful life. However, if we practice inappropriate action we can expect infelicitous results (Galatians 6:7–9).

Blaming God for all the bad things that occur in our lives is a sure sign that we do not understand God and His Word. There are folks who believe God is all-powerful and can cause good things to come to them, and when He doesn't, they blame Him. It is so easy to blame someone else for our lack of integrity, laziness, and incongruous lifestyle.

We are promised an abundant life if we are willing to find how God's laws work. They are available for anyone to study. God has even promised to help us obey those laws (Romans 8:26). Perhaps there is a flaw in our character that hampers our following one of God's laws for success. If we will go to Him in faith and admit our inadequacy, He will supernaturally help our infirmity.

We really have no one to blame but ourselves if we do not have an abundant life. It's available. Jesus said, "I am come that you might have life and that you might have it more abundantly" (John 10:10). He was not talking about heaven. He was talking about now. Note that He said we *might* have abundant life. Why the "might"? Because it's up to us whether we are willing to obey His laws. It is the law of life.

(CHAPTER FIFTEEN)

The Snubbing Post

> Stand ye still and see the salvation of the Lord. (2 CHRONICLES 20:17)

Many places in God's Word we find the reminder to stand still and see God perform an act of deliverance. This promise is strongest when we are encountering conflict in a relationship. Disagreements occur, possibly causing a myriad of scars. Dissension comes between nations, religions, businesses, families, and individuals. It is not a question of whether it will happen, but a question of *when*. Jesus Christ said, "Woe unto the world because of offenses! Such things must come, but woe to the man through whom they come" (Matthew 18:7).

Because it is inevitable that conflict will arise, Jesus Christ addressed how His followers should handle this sin. I am dedicating this chapter to the topic of how we should conduct ourselves when disputes transpire. I will explain the title "The Snubbing Post."

Several years ago I was accused of wrong conduct in business. It was a slur that was unfounded and later was proved to be groundless. But while I was going through it my reputation was at risk. My business was insurance and investments. Integrity and fiduciary responsibility were very important to my name. Also, I was on the board of our church and had a high profile, as a Christian, in the city. This caused a negative reflection on the church. From my perspective it was harmful to the kingdom of God.

I tried locating the source of conflict and found it to be a rumor originating with an individual who was angry toward our church. Being jealous of my success in the insurance business, he thought it would be a good way to hurt the church and me as well.

The rumor was spreading. Bad news spreads faster than good news. People are attracted to evil—it makes for juicy gossip. That's why tragic news sells newspapers and makes good television ratings. It's innate in humanity to believe the worst.

Although the rumor was affecting my business, it was not my primary concern. The foundation of my life was Matthew 6:33—"Seek first the kingdom of God"—and the rumor was having an effect on God's reputation through the way it was making me look to the public.

Along with my pastor and church friends, I beseeched God for the best way to approach this conflict. God gave us a solution so profound that it has been a road map for handling conflicts ever since. As God does so much of the time, He used a natural (supernaturally natural) example for the answer.

My family and I lived on a 160-acre farm, raising horses and cattle. At times we would train a young horse to accept the halter. I had a short telephone pole set in concrete so that it wouldn't move when a horse pulled away from it. The horse would strain against the rope, but the post stayed firm. Eventually, the horse learned to stop trying and accepted the halter. We called the post "a snubbing post" because it refused to move.

God used that metaphor to teach me how to handle a rumor. When rumors are flying, they can be compared to feathers turned loose in the wind—impossible to catch. We become frustrated and angry trying, which only makes the situation much worse.

Rumors are illusory. Their origin is nearly impossible to trace, as they don't have a systematic beginning. Gossip is a rumor's main function. The rumor or gossip may incorporate a smattering of truth—enough to lend credibility—but the small amount of truth will be twisted to fit the rumor. This action is Satan's favorite tool to destroy and rob a person of his or her most prized possession: reputation and character (John 10:10).

God's remedy for this problem is to stand still and see the salvation of the Lord. This is not your battle, it's God fight (Exodus 14:13–14; 2 Timothy 4:18; Acts 5:38–39). God said to me: "I want you to be that snubbing post. Stand firm. If you don't move, then I have something to work with. But if you move and get involved, it shall be like a quagmire—nothing to work toward. Don't take it out of my hands."

Retaliation is the norm for humanity. Revenge is a common desire when conflict occurs. Proving that we are right and the other side wrong, is our greatest desire. But when we search our hearts, we realize that it is pride motivating us.

A word of caution when dealing with this subject: if the child of God has earned an accusation, the requirement changes and something must be done to correct the indictment. We can't wait for God to accomplish something that is our responsibility. Many people do. They believe or hope that God will somehow correct the charge.

There are times when we do harm to others but do nothing to correct the situation, depending upon all being forgotten. This kind of action indicates a lack of integrity, weak character, and laziness. The Word of God frowns on such methods of dealing with relationships and has harsh words for those that do such things (1 Corinthians 11:28–32).

If we truly desire to resolve a conflict, we must lay aside all semblances of pride and self-serving attitude. We must give the opposing party an opportunity to air its grievances. Our attitude should be one of understanding the opposite view.

We may not be able to accept their view, but we have given them an opportunity to share their version of the conflict. We may be able to see why they feel the way they do.

Unless the opposing party is completely self-centered, they will in turn give you the opportunity to share your side of the conflict. Generally, the dispute can be settled amicably. Both sides may come away with an understanding that conserves the relationship.

The format we have been proposing is not pleasing to human nature. It does not lead to a win-lose proposition; instead, it facilitates a solution with peace and understanding. This is a principle that Jesus Christ ordains for His followers (Matthew 5:43–48).

This method of conflict resolution works where there is bona fide interest on both sides. Every effort should be made to bring both parties to the table of reconciliation. It helps to have a mediator to facilitate a fair and calm exchange of views. It is important for the mediator to understand—not to make a decision or a judgment. The mediator is only a facilitator.

When the conflict is based upon rumor and research reveals only falsehood, then it is best to leave it in the hands of God. In this sort of condition it is generally an act of Satan to accuse, destroy, and rob a person or persons, or a work of God (John 10:10). The battle is against God. Do not get in God's way by retaliating.

When Jesus Christ was accused by the chief priests and elders, He did not say a word. Why didn't He defend Himself? It was because the battle was God's fight.

Everything that happened during His trial was trumped up in order to have Him crucified. It was God's plan to bring about our redemption (Matthew 27:12–14).

The cross of Jesus Christ became a "snubbing post." People have tried to move the cross; they have fought wars over it, tried to move it with psychology, and by every means they could devise, but the cross stands firm. If humankind wants God's favor, then they must come to the cross. It will not move.

We are soldiers of the cross, as born-again believers; we seek the kingdom of God in the way we live. We can expect the enemy to accuse us from time to time. We must always be aware of his methods. We must also be on guard that we do not give him an opportunity for accusations that are true.

If the accusations are true, then do what you can to correct them. If they are not true, then stand still and see the salvation of the Lord. Judging our own action is extremely difficult. We have a tendency to justify everything we do. The honest evaluation of our own actions brings God joy and He rewards us for doing so. When we adjudicate our own endeavors, then it isn't necessary for God to correct us (1 Corinthians 11:31–32).

This is the reason God called David "a man after My own heart" (Acts 13:22). David was not without wrongdoing in his life; on the contrary, he did things that were despicable. He committed adultery with Bathsheba (2 Samuel 11:4). Then he had her husband killed so that he could have her as his wife (2 Samuel 11:15). Yet God called him a man after His own heart because David was quick to admit his failure and asked God for forgiveness (Psalm 51).

If we are honest with ourselves and with God, it leads to a clean heart in Christ Jesus, as well as a much healthier life.

(CHAPTER SIXTEEN)

Vessel to Honor, Vessel to Dishonor

> In a great house there are not only vessels of gold and of silver, but also of wood and of earth; and some to honor, and some to dishonor. (2 TIMOTHY 2:20)

This chapter could be classified as a recap of all previous chapters, designed to bring our focus clearly into understanding why Jesus Christ called us out of the world for the purpose of showing the world that God is worthy of trust, obedience, and praise (1 Peter 2:9: "But you are a chosen people, a royal priesthood, a holy nation, a people belonging to God, that you may declare the praises of him who called you out of darkness into his wonderful light").

The Bible resorts to familiar analogies so that we can relate to something we understand. We can readily identify with a house being built with various types of materials. Some materials are valuable and lasting; others are flimsy, of poor quality, and prone to burn.

The biblical symbolism of a great house is a metaphor for the church of Jesus Christ, the kingdom of Heaven on earth. Vessels of honor and vessels of dishonor are typologies of people within the church that represent Jesus Christ.

Honorable people bring a positive personification of Christ and

His kingdom, whereas dishonorable folks bring an igniminious representation of God's kingdom and His church. Venal people are easily corrupted when they are confronted with persecution, affliction, the deceitfulness of riches and lust for things (Mark 4:17–19).

Vessels are favorite typologies of God's Word to illustrate people or nations that God uses for His purpose. God told Jeremiah to watch a potter making a vessel; one vessel is marred in the hands of the potter and is remade into a useful vessel (Jeremiah 18:1–10). In this instance, God is referring to the nation of Israel. If Israel will respond to God's Word, in obedience, the potter will make them into a useful vessel. Of course, Israel refused to conform to God's Word, so they were set aside, and another vessel (the church) was created for the purpose of witnessing to the world.

In the metaphor of the church being a great house and people being vessels, there is a significant difference in the way God deals with dishonorable vessels than He did Israel. Although He holds them accountable and will judge their actions, He does not completely set them aside; they may not be eternally lost, unless they deny their faith in Jesus Christ (1 Corinthians 3:15: "If it is burned up, he will suffer loss; he himself will be saved, but only as one escaping through the flames"), but they lose the rewards designated as theirs. Losing rewards would be a sad outcome, as everyone wants what God has planned for them.

We note a significant difference when reading about God's action with Israel in Jeremiah, where the nation is set aside because of disobedience, from what we read in 2 Timothy 2:15–21 or 1 Corinthians 3:11–15, where God is addressing the church and the people being disobedient. We do not see God casting the whole church aside as His emissary, only the individuals who insist upon harming the quality of the church.

There is a warning and an encouragement for troublemakers in the church to rethink their actions and make changes for the better. If they purge themselves of such actions, they can be vessels of honor and useful for God's kingdom (2 Timothy 2:21: "If a man cleanses himself from [ignoble purposes], he will be an instrument for noble purposes, made holy, useful to the Master and prepared to do any good work"). It's important to note that God knows who is faithful and who is not (2 Timothy 2:15).

The fundamental purpose of this chapter is to emphasize the importance of considering our actions within the church that we attend. Am I a detriment, or am I an asset who makes a positive contribution to the leadership and body of the church? I realize that this question can be subjective. That is why we must depend upon God's Word and the Holy Spirit for our direction. Wisdom and common sense also do not hurt.

When we are confronted with a situation in which we are in conflict with someone or disagree with something that has taken place, how should we react? The answer to this question can be so complex that it is impossible to respond definitively. It is possible, however, to give some direction:

- Is the conflict personal; that is, it is between me and another party? (If so, then a meeting between that person and me may be the answer.)
- Is the difference between the pastor and me? (If so, a private meeting between the pastor and me may suffice.)
- Am I in disagreement with a point of teaching? (If so, I must consider whether I am in a leadership capacity. If I am not, I must not cause a problem with my feedback.)

There could be so many different combinations concerning the conflict that it takes godly wisdom to determine what we should do. If we truly want the direction of the Holy Spirit, then we must not have an agenda of our own. We must consider what is best for the body of Christ.

Seeking first the kingdom of God and His righteousness is the key to being a vessel of honor.

(CHAPTER SEVENTEEN)

Security

Humanity has searched for knowledge of the future ever since the dawn of time, but God has reserved such knowledge for Himself. We humans felt that God was holding out on us for selfish reasons (Genesis 3:4–5: "'You will not surely die,' the serpent said to the woman. 'For God knows that when you eat of it your eyes will be opened, and you will be like God, knowing good and evil'"). Therein lies the fundamental conflict between God and us. We desire to be God and to be in charge of our own fate. But in order to do that, we must know the future.

Lucifer (later known as Satan) entertained the same philosophy (Isaiah 14:12–17). In his determination to be greater than God (Isaiah 14:13: "I will ascend into heaven, I will exalt my throne above the stars of God"), Lucifer, along with one-third of the angels, waged an all-out war against God, but he was defeated and banished from God's presence (Revelation 12:1–9). Satan became God's archenemy. He could not succeed against God, so he went after God's supreme creation—humankind.

Satan uses the same tactics on us that destroyed his relationship with God. We, too, desire either to be equal with God or ignore Him completely. However, something we need is to know the future in order to secure it—but that knowledge belongs to God alone.

Adam and Eve traded away our supervisory position to Satan in the Garden of Eden. Because human beings lost that position, a human being must win it back, so Jesus Christ, as a man, defeated Satan in the earthly arena through his submission to the will of the Father in Gethsemane, and his subsequent death on the cross and resurrection. It was a legal victory, giving God the opportunity to send the Holy Spirit to be resident in each believer (Acts 2:4). Receiving the Holy Spirit activates the recipient into the "church" of Jesus Christ.

Each believer has access to many benefits that were lost in the Garden of Eden, one of which is *security*. We are not given concrete information with which to make decisions that affect our security, but we *are* given God's Word, His assurance, that all is well with the future (Romans 8:28; Jeremiah 29:11–12).

Having confidence in sources of information is a premium today. Investment companies, the media, government agencies and representatives, the courts, pharmaceutical houses, and numerous institutions have shaken our trust. When fiduciary institutions prove unreliable, life takes on a quicksand type of insecurity—nothing feels solid (Matthew 7:26: "'Everyone who hears these words of mine and does not put them into practice is like a foolish man who built his house on sand'").

The believer, abiding in the secret place, has access to wisdom from God, the one who knows all things (James 1:5; Proverbs 3:4–6). Trusting God is an exercise in faith. Material life may look rocky and full of misadventure, but if we take our guidance from God, the outcome will be victory.

Friends, family members, and trusted advisers will sometimes let us down if the temptation becomes too great, leaving us bewildered and disappointed. Believers have assurance that Jesus Christ will never leave or forsake them (Hebrews 13:5–6: "God said, 'Never will I leave you; never will I forsake you.' So we say with confidence, 'The Lord is my helper; I will not be afraid. What can man do to me?'").

Occasionally we encounter situations in which, through our stupidity and bad judgment, we cause destructive things to happen to our lives. When this occurs we are left with no recourse but to pay the penalty. Even our friends desert us, and the courts find us guilty. We must stand alone. What a horrible feeling.

Take heart! Even though we must pay our dues, whether to friends or society, we still have "a friend who sticks closer than a brother" (Proverbs 18:24). When the court finds us guilty and passes sentence, there is still hope for a better future, because the believer has access to a higher court, one that does not demand justice but has mercy. That is when we can appreciate God's invitation to come to the "Throne of God, in Christ Jesus" (Hebrews 4:14–16)—a throne of mercy and grace.

Peace is the cry of the day, but it seems to evade us at every turn. Today, as I am writing this chapter on security and peace, I have received word that my friend and physician has committed suicide. What a waste, how sad. Life can be cruel when Christ is left out of the equation. Jesus Christ has promised peace, direction, and insight (John 14:1–34).

I have referred to the believer "dwelling in the secret place," but what is that secret place? Does God select who abides in the coveted position? How can I know whether I qualify? It sounds as if I can be a believer and yet not dwell in the secret place.

I believe this is the crux of the Matthew 6:33 principle. The secret place is a place of dedication to God in Jesus Christ, where believers are concerned with God's desires (will) and place His agenda above their own. Romans 8:28 validates this concept: everything works to our good, if we love God and are called according to His purpose.

Invitation to the secret place is open to whosoever will come (Romans 10:13). "For there is no partiality with God" (Romans 2:11). The qualification rests upon the believer's obedience to the will of God. Perfection is not a qualification; if it were, there wouldn't be a single human being in the secret place. We all have faults; we all stumble and fall and make mistakes. The secret is our heart's desire, our bent or mind-set. Jesus Christ is our righteousness, but He will not force us to be obedient.

A person can be born again, therefore, a child of God in Christ Jesus, and still not dwell in the secret place. That person's life isn't blessed with all the rewards that would otherwise be available (1 Corinthians 3:12–15).

The choice is ours: "This day I call heaven and earth as witnesses against you that I have set before you life and death, blessings and curses. Now choose life, so that you and your children may live and that you may love the Lord your God, listen to his voice, and hold fast to him. For the Lord is your life, and he will give you many years in the land he swore to give to your fathers, Abraham, Isaac and Jacob" (Deuteronomy 30:19–20). Seek first the kingdom of God and His righteousness and all these things shall be added unto us.

May the Holy Spirit be your guide and your security.

To order additional copies of *The Matthew 6:33 Principle*:

Web: www.itascabooks.com

Phone: 1-800-901-3480

Fax: Copy and fill out the form below with credit card information. Fax to 763-398-0198.

Mail: Copy and fill out the form below. Mail with check or credit card information to:

Syren Book Company
5120 Cedar Lake Road
Minneapolis, MN 55416

Order Form

Copies	Title / Author	Price	Totals
	The Matthew 6:33 Principle / Sam Jordan	$11.95	$
	Subtotal		$
	7% sales tax (MN only)		$
	Shipping and handling, first copy		$ 4.00
	Shipping and handling, ___ add'l copies @$1.00 ea.		$
	TOTAL TO REMIT		$

Payment Information:

__ Check Enclosed __ Visa/MasterCard		
Card number:	Expiration date:	
Name on card:		
Billing address:		
City:	State:	Zip:
Signature :	Date:	

Shipping Information:

__ Same as billing address __ Other (enter below)		
Name:		
Address:		
City:	State:	Zip: